LOT Polish

Wings of Centra

JOZEF MOLS

AIRLINES SERIES, VOLUME 7

Published by Key Books
An imprint of Key Publishing Ltd
PO Box 100
Stamford
Lincs PE19 1XQ

www.keypublishing.com

The rights of Jozef Mols to be identified as the author of this book has been asserted in accordance with the Copyright, Designs and Patents Act 1988 Sections 77 and 78.

Copyright © Jozef Mols, 2022

ISBN 978 1 80282 260 1

Typeset by SJmagic DESIGN SERVICES, India.

Contents

Introduction and Acknowledgements

The history of LOT Polish Airlines is as fascinating as the history of Poland itself; a country that only gained its independence in 1918, after 123 years of partitions, though this independence would prove to be very fragile. The first truly Polish airline was established in Poznań in 1921 for the duration of the Poznań Fair. Strangely enough, later airline initiatives within Poland actually have their origins outside the country. For example, German investors started up airlines in the Free City of Danzig – a semi-autonomous city-state that existed between 1920 and 1939, which was administered by the League of Nations. When airlines were established within Poland itself, these merged with the companies from Danzig to form Aerolot, the company that would later become the core of LOT Polish Airlines. Aerolot was set to expand rapidly in Europe, but the German occupation of Poland during World War Two put an end to its success. After the war, LOT could start up operations again, but this time it would be under Soviet control, as Russian troops occupied Poland. It would only be after the fall of the Berlin Wall that LOT could more freely add modern Western equipment to its fleet (the airline did already use some Convairs and Vickers Viscounts on specific European routes). LOT had to adapt like a chameleon to its always-changing political and economic habitat, and the many challenges the airline faced and had to overcome make its story one worth telling.

The author wishes to thank all photographers who made their pictures available for publication in this book. Special gratitude goes to the employees of the National Digital Archives in Poland, who painstakingly collected, scanned, processed and labelled hundreds of thousands of photographs and made them available to journalists and historians. Furthermore, I wish to thank my partner, Marianne Van Leuvenhaege, for proofreading the manuscript of this book. And, of course, my gratitude also goes to Key for publishing and distributing this book.

Jozef Mols
Wommelgem, Belgium
14 February 2022

Chapter 1
Some Polish History

When one studies the history of Polish civil aviation, it will quickly become clear that its origins can be found in Germany. This is, of course, the result of the rather complex history of the country itself. Therefore, it is necessary to understand this history in order to fully appreciate the birth and evolution of its airline.

Historical records on the Polish state begin with the rule of Duke Mieszko I, which commenced sometime before 963 and continued until his death in 992. He completed the unification of different tribal lands, a move that was fundamental to the country's existence, and he, and the rulers that came after him, succeeded in creating strong national identity. However, between 1002 and 1018, the country would fight prolonged wars with the Kingdom of Germany, and, in the following centuries, as the resources of the early Polish state were overstretched from its rulers' expansionist ambitions, the collapse of the monarchy grew nearer. This, combined with internal fragmentation, eroded the monarchical structures in the 12th and 13th centuries.[1]

In 1226, a duke invited the Teutonic Knights to help him fight the Baltic Prussian pagans. The Teutonic Order destroyed the Prussians but kept their lands, which resulted in centuries of warfare between Poland and the Knights, and later between Poland and the German Prussian state. Attempts to reunite Polish lands continued, however, and, in 1295, Duke Przemysł II became the first ruler since Boleslaw II (who ruled 1076–79) to be crowned king of Poland, although he had to rule over a limited territory (territories included the Duchies of Lesser Poland, Greater Poland, Silesia, Masovia and Sandomierz). In 1308, the Teutonic Knights seized Gdańsk and the surrounding region of Pomerelia. After the Polish royal line died out, Poland came under the rule of Louis I of Hungary and the Capetian House of Anjou, which presided over a union of Hungary and Poland that lasted until 1382.

In 1374, Louis granted the Polish nobility the Privilege of Koszyce in order to assure his daughter, Jadwiga, would ascend to the throne on his death. When she married Grand Duke Jogaila of Lithuania, this enabled the Grand Duke to become king of Poland. In 1454, Royal Prussia was incorporated into Poland, resulting in a 13-year war between Polish forces and resistance fighters in Royal Prussia. The reign of Sigismund II gave rise to the Union of Lublin in 1569, an ultimate fulfilment of the union of Poland and Lithuania. This agreement transferred Ukraine from the Grand Duchy of Lithuania to Polish control and established a Polish-Lithuanian Commonwealth, which became a federal state. The union would become an influential participant in European affairs and a vital cultural entity, as the Commonwealth was one of the largest and most populous states in Europe.

When the Polish nobility organised the first 'free elections' of royals in 1573, Henry of Valois became the winner, but he fled Poland when news arrived of the vacancy of the French throne to which he was the heir. The royal elections increased foreign influence in the Commonwealth, as foreign powers sought to manipulate the Polish nobility to place candidates amicable to their interests. A period under the Swedish House of Vasa began in the Commonwealth in 1587. The first two kings of Poland repeatedly vied for accession to the throne of Sweden, which was a constant source of distraction for the affairs of the Commonwealth. As a result of warfare with Russia, Poland could expand its eastern territories, but the goal of taking over the Russian throne was not achieved. As a result of foreign invasions and domestic uprisings against serfdom, the nobles' democracy fell into decline, marking the end of the 'Polish Golden Age' (generally considered from the late 15th century through to King

Sigismund II's death in 1572). After an uprising of Cossacks in the southeastern regions of the country, the Ukrainian rebels declared themselves subjects of the Tsar of Russia. In the end, Ukraine would be divided between Poland and Russia. In the first half of the 18th century, Poland ceased to be an active player in international politics. The Commonwealth with Lithuania was disintegrated in 1772 at the instigation of Frederick the Great of Prussia, who divided parts of the Commonwealth among Prussia, Austria and Russia, in what is known as the First Partition of Poland.

When, in 1788, King Stanisław August of Poland passed a constitution, this generated strong opposition from the conservative circles of the upper nobility. The constitution was indeed a reformist document, sympathetic to the ideals of the French Revolution. The local nobility appealed to Empress Catherine of Russia to intervene, resulting in a Polish-Russian war. The Polish king had to capitulate, and Russian allied forces took over the government. In 1793, the Second Partition of Poland took place, which further reduced the territory and rendered it incapable of independent existence. In 1795, Polish reformers worked on a national insurrection under the leadership of Tadeuz Kosciuszko, a Polish veteran of the American Revolution. The insurrection, however, proved incapable of generating foreign assistance and was suppressed by the combined forces of Russia and Prussia. For the third time, a partition of the territory would take place. Although no sovereign Polish state existed between 1795 and 1918, the idea of Polish independence was kept alive throughout the 19th and early 20th century.

After Napoleon's initial defeat, a new European order was established at the Congress of Vienna in 1814. The congress implemented a new partition scheme, which took into account the support of Polish forces during the war against Napoleon. In exchange for this support, the Kingdom of Poland came into existence with the support of the great nations, Prussia, Russia, France, Austria and the United Kingdom. This kingdom was joined to the Russian Empire in a personal union under the Russian tsar, but it was allowed to have its own constitution and army.

The outbreak of World War One offered Poles unexpected hopes for achieving independence as a result of the turbulence that engulfed the empires (Russia, Germany, Austria) that had been responsible for the partitioning of Poland. The monarchies of these empires were all dissolved by the end of the war, and many of their territories were dispersed into new political units. When, on 11 November 1918, the Republic of Poland regained its independence after 123 years of partitions, pilots who had taken an active part in the Great War returned to their homeland. Their experience was not wasted. At that time, Warsaw, Poznań, Kraków, Lviv and Gdańsk (known then as the Free City of Danzig) were the most important cities, and therefore became of much interest to potential air transport investors.

It is nearly impossible to understand the history of aviation in Poland without some knowledge about the political situation and history of Danzig (Gdańsk). The Free City of Danzig was a semi-autonomous city-state that existed between 1920 and 1939, consisting of the Baltic Sea port of Danzig and nearly 200 towns and villages in the surrounding areas. Many of these were primarily inhabited by Germans. The Free City was created on 15 November 1920 in accordance with the 1919 Treaty of Versailles at the end of World War One. According to the Treaty, the region was to remain separated from the post-war German Republic and from the newly independent Polish Republic. Therefore, the Free City was placed under League of Nations protection. To facilitate trade in the region, it was put into a binding customs union with Poland. Poland also obtained some rights regarding communication as well as the railway and port facilities in the city.[2]

The first traces of Polish aviation could be found in the city of Danzig, even before it became a Free City after World War One. For the occasion of the Danziger Fest-und Flugwoche (Danzig Festival and Flight Week) in 1910, an airfield was built for Hans Grade (a Prussian pilot) and Emil Jeannin (a pilot from Elzas-Lotharingen) to demonstrate their aircraft. Also in 1910, Friedrich Sigismund of Prussia built an airfield in Langfuhr, near Danzig. During World War One, this facility would be used by Prussian pilots. After the war, the airfield came under the control of the Free City of Danzig. A few months after the creation of the Free City, the Danziger Luftpost started up its activities with a fleet of Rumpler C.I aircraft. Together with Lloyd Ostflug, the Danziger Luftpost would operate mail services on the route linking Berlin via Schneidemühl to Danzig and further to Königsberg. A month later, passenger services were started, using a Junkers F 13 aircraft.[3]

The first fully domestic airline in Poland was established in Poznań in 1921, with the purpose of supporting participants and visitors to the first Poznań Fair. The organising committee decided to launch an air connection between Poznań, Warsaw and Gdańsk for the duration of the fair. Therefore, on 10 May 1921, the Aero-Targ Communication Society was established. The organising committee allocated a total of 5 million Polish marks to finance the start-up. Aero-Targ established cooperation with the Gdańsk transport company Danziger Luftpost, from which it borrowed six Junkers F 13 aircraft. The flights started on 28 May 1921, on the opening day of the fair, and would operate until the closing date on 5 June 1921. During this period, the airline made 58 flights on the Poznań–Warsaw–Poznań route and 30 flights on the Poznań–Gdańsk–Poznań route, transporting about 100 passengers and 6,600lb (3,000kg) of freight (mainly air mail). The Poczta Polska (Polish Post) used the airline to send airmail and issued a special series of stamps on this occasion. However, the airline could not make a profit, and the organising committee of the fair could not recuperate its initial investment. Nevertheless, the venture was considered to be a success.[4]

Before World War Two, Poland was an important producer and exporter of crude oil. Many of the oilfields were located in Galicia, which was ranked fourth in the world as an oil producer by the beginning of the 20th century. Ignacy Wygard, Bronisław Dunin-Żuchowski and Kazimierz Unruch, the owners of Fanto – the largest oil-producing company in Galicia – decided to set up a second Polish airline, Aerolloyd, in 1922. Their main intention was to enable oil barons like themselves to travel quickly between the Boryslaw and Drohobycz oilfields, Warsaw (where the company had its headquarters) and the Port of Danzig, through which their products were exported.

Norddeutscher Lloyd, which had earlier set up Deutscher Aero Lloyd with a Danzig airmail subsidiary, Lloyd Ostflug, had to limit its operations because of French pressure. This pressure stemmed from the Treaty of Versailles, which limited all German activities in the aviation sector. As a result, Norddeutscher Lloyd, which wanted a presence in Danzig, gave its financial backing to Aerolloyd. Aircraft from Lloyd Ostflug were therefore leased to Aerolloyd. The Polish airline enjoyed subsidies from the Polish government, and it could operate its aircraft from military airfields in Poland free of charge. From its base in the Free City of Danzig, the airline operated a Danzig–Warsaw–Lwów service with a later extension to Kraków in 1924. In 1925, the route would be further extended to Vienna, and, in 1926, to Brno.[5]

From its incorporation, the airline came under pressure from the Polish government to 'Polonise' its staff and shareholders and to buy aircraft from Poland's allies rather than from Germany. Changing aircraft suppliers, however, was a problem as Junkers' prices were much lower than those of other manufacturers. Therefore, the company decided to stick with German aircraft, but bought them from Junkers' Swedish subsidiary, rather than from the Dessau factory. As a gesture towards the government, the airline was renamed Aerolot in 1925, as the 'Lloyd' in its previous name was heavily reminiscent of Germany. Former German shareholders were also bought out. Aerolot moved its headquarters from the Free City of Danzig to Mokotow Airport in Warsaw. In 1926, a Warsaw–Łódź route was opened. Initially, the airline had used a fleet of six Junkers F 13 aircraft, leased from Lloyd Ostflug and flown by pilots from the Junkers factory. With time, they were replaced with Polish pilots who trained in Dessau. In 1925, Aerolot even considered buying a three-motor Junkers G-23W floatplane, to be used on an intended Danzig–Malmö–Copenhagen service, but the aircraft was returned to Junkers after some trial flights. By 1926, ten more F 13s were added to the fleet.

Of course, Aerolot had competitors. In 1925, Aero Sp.z.o.o was established in Poznań, which later became a joint stock company under the name of Aero Komunikna SA, with a base at the Ławica airport. In contrast with Aerolot, Aero Komunikna bought its aircraft in France. A total of two used and three new Farman F.70 aircraft were obtained. On 21 May 1925, the airline operated a series of propaganda flights over the city of Poznań. The first commercial flights took place on 23 May 1925 on the Poznań–Warsaw route. Subsequent flights were also made with a stopover in Łódź. In 1928, Aero purchased six Dutch Fokker F.VIIa/1m aircraft: the first real transport aircraft with a high level of safety and comfort. By the end of 1928, the airline had transported 3,200 passengers.

In 1927, Aerolot initiated a Polish Air Union, which included Aerolot itself and also its main competitors, Aero Sp.z.o.o and Silesian Air Society. Two years later, the Polish government nationalised and merged all three companies to form Linji Lotnicze LOT Sp.z.o.o.[6] By this time, the Polish government had studied the development of aviation in the United States, where over 50 private airlines were operating. In order to prevent chaos in Poland and to ensure uniform standards, a programme was launched at the Civil Aviation Department of the Ministry of Communications regarding changes in the Polish Aviation Communication. This programme included the liquidation of all private aviation companies and their replacement by one single state-owned airline, Polskie Linie Lotnicze LOT S.A. (LOT Polish Airlines, abbreviated in this work to LOT).

Above: The Aero-Targ Communication Society only operated flights during the Poznań Fair, and for this occasion, the Poczta Polska (Polish Post) issued a special series of stamps. (National Digital Archive Poland)

Left: In 1981, the Polish Post issued special air mail stamps to commemorate the 60th birthday of air mail in Poland. (National Digital Archive Poland)

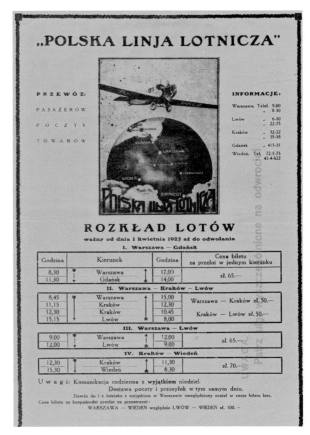

Right: An Aerolot timetable, issued in 1925.
(National Digital Archive Poland)

Below: The Aerolot office in Warsaw in 1923.
(National Digital Archive Poland)

Above: Aerolot could lease Junkers aircraft from Deutscher Aero Lloyd's Danzig subsidiary, Lloyd Ostflug. (National Digital Archive Poland)

Left: An Aerolot Junkers F 13, leased in Danzig from Deutscher Aero Lloyd. (National Digital Archive Poland)

Below: A Junkers F 13 from Deutscher Aero Lloyd in Danzig. (National Digital Archive Poland)

Aerolot's competitor, Aero Komunikna, obtained French Farman aircraft and also considered the Potez 32. (National Digital Archive Poland)

Aero Komunikna also used the Fokker F.VII A one-engined passenger aircraft. (National Digital Archive Poland)

Chapter 2
The Interbellum: Establishing an Airline

When, in 1929, the private airlines of Poland were merged into a single state-controlled airline, LOT Polish Airlines, their fleets were also merged. On 1 January 1929, LOT had a fleet of 15 Junkers F 13s, together with six Fokker F.VIIa single-engined aircraft. The French-built aircraft that previously belonged to Aero Komunikna were not taken over by the new airline, as they were no longer in good flying condition.

The Polish government, which was the main shareholder of LOT (86 per cent of the shares, with the rest divided between the Province of Silesia and the city of Poznań), was also interested in building upon the aviation industry within Poland itself. To that effect, the airline purchased a licence to build the Fokker F.VII with three engines in Poland. Production of the aircraft was commissioned to Plage & Laśkiewicz, Poland's first aerospace manufacturer, in Lublin in 1929–30. The contract stipulated a total of 31 aircraft would be built, including 11 civilian versions and 20 aircraft for the military. The passenger version took ten passengers, whereas the transport version would be able to carry 2,200lb to 3,300lb (1,000kg to 1,500kg) of freight. The aircraft had Lorraine-Dietrich LD-12B inline engines. Later, the engines would be replaced by Skoda-built Wright Whirlwind J5As. Under the terms of the contract with Fokker, one licence-built aircraft had to be delivered to Belgium. It was delivered with the serial OO-AIG.[1]

From the inception of LOT, the emphasis was on advertising and implementing new connections. Numerous posters and folders were distributed in Polish cities. Sightseeing flights were organised in Warsaw. Flights from Warsaw to Katowice and Bydgoszcz were started in 1931. Back in November 1929, a competition for a logo for the new company had been announced. The winner was a design by Gronowski, which depicted a stylised crane. In 1931, the symbol was officially recognised as the company's emblem. During the General National Exhibition in 1929 in Poznań, special flights between Warsaw and Poznań were launched. The first connection outside Poland was the Warsaw–Bucharest route, operated from 1 April 1930 onwards. Soon, Athens, Beirut and Helsinki were added to the route network.[2] Soon, LOT had the second largest network of connections (after Air France), and there was an intention to further expand the network, even to destinations outside the continent. In the meantime, LOT had become member of the International Air Transport Association (IATA) in 1930.

Indigenous vs imported design

While the licensed production of the Fokker F.VII was going on, the government was also considering not only production of foreign-designed aircraft but also the indigenous design of passenger aircraft. In 1927, the government had held a design competition for a domestic airliner, which attracted several entries. Plage & Laśkiewicz (generally known as Lublin, after the location of its headquarters) offered a design by Jerzy Rudlicki, intended to replace the four-seat Junkers F 13. This design, the Lublin R-XVI, was based upon an earlier bomber design by the same engineer and owed much to Fokker design practice. The rectangular-section fuselage was of welded steel tube construction, rigid forward and wire-braced aft with fabric covering. Passenger accommodation comprised two side-by-side reclining seats forward and a bench seat for two aft. There was also a baggage hold beneath the cockpit. Power was provided by a single Skoda-built J-5 Whirlwind 9-cylinder air-cooled radial piston engine of 160kW (220hp). The aircraft made its first flight in February 1932, and, in the middle of that year, it went to LOT for trial flights on mail and non-scheduled operations. The test models proved in need of some modifications, and LOT decided it could not wait for these to be undertaken. Although LOT did not buy this model, it went into service with the Polish Medical Aviation Research Centre and the Red Cross.[3,4] Later on, these aircraft would be used during the German invasion of Poland in 1939.

Despite the purchase of the Fokker F.VIIb/3m aircraft, the Polish government also wanted a Polish-designed passenger aircraft for ten passengers. Polish engineer Zygmunt Bruner, working in the French Bernard works, won the competition with an all-metal, high-wing, three-engined monoplane, somewhat similar to the Ford Trimotor. PZL (Państwowe Zakłady Lotnicze, State Aviation Works) decided to take over its development, and a group of Polish engineers were sent to Paris to work on the design. Detailed technical drawings were subsequently made by PZL in Warsaw in 1930. The PZL.4 had a crew of two, and it offered room for ten passengers in three compartments in the fuselage. The cabin had place for luggage behind the seats and below the floor. Three 9-cylinder Polish Skoda J5A radial engines mounted in the fuselage nose and in the wing nacelles provided take-off power. The prototype made its first flight in January 1932. From autumn 1932 to 1935, it was evaluated by LOT, but the airline found it unsatisfactory – the empty weight was larger than the design specifications, which decreased the performance of the aircraft. The aircraft was withdrawn from service in 1936 and scrapped in 1937.[5]

The only Polish company to achieve any success in obtaining orders for Polish-designed transport aircraft was PWS (Podlaska Wytwórnia Samolotów, Podlaska Aircraft Factory), although even these orders were small. The PWS-20T, as it was originally known, was designed as a private venture. The Polish Ministry of Transport decided to order three for LOT. With a ski undercarriage, the PWS-20T made its first flight on 12 March 1929. The aircraft was powered by a Skoda-built Lorraine-Dietrich 12E 12-cylinder water-cooled engine. The partly enclosed cockpit had side-by-side seats, and the cabin had six fixed and two folding seats. Later on, the cockpit was fully enclosed, and the cabin would receive four fixed seats on each side. The PWS-20 went to LOT for evaluation in the autumn of 1929, and the airline asked for some changes, including a new wide-track undercarriage. This new version got the type designation PWS-20bis. It began its proving flights over the Warsaw–Bucharest route, and the aircraft would later be used as a freighter on the Warsaw–Lwów route. However, LOT found it too difficult to operate a few PWS20 aircraft along the fleet of Fokkers, so the type was withdrawn from service in the second half of 1931. However, PWS did not give up. It offered the PWS-24 design as a replacement for the Junkers F 13 on domestic routes. This model made its first flight in August 1931. In April 1932, it went to LOT for evaluation flights. In the spring of that year, the airline ordered five aircraft, which entered service in May 1933 on the Warsaw–Poznań route. Although the PWS-24 proved successful, it was regarded as slow, and as a result LOT asked for more powerful engines. The Skoda/Wright Whirlwind J5 of 220hp was replaced by a Lorraine 9NA Algol 9-cylinder radial engine, but ultimately the Pratt & Whitney Wasp Junior TB would be chosen. In 1936, the aircraft would be converted to aerial photography and used until the outbreak of World War Two.[6,7]

In 1934, LOT was allocated headquarters at Warsaw-Okęcie, where a modern airport had been built, complete with technical facilities, hangars, workshops and warehouses. As the Polish aviation industry had not been very successful in providing new aircraft for LOT, the airline decided in 1935 to purchase three Douglas DC-2 aircraft. On 23 November 1937, one of them crashed in Bulgaria, killing all people on board. After the German invasion of Poland, one DC-2 was interned in Riga, whereas the second remaining aircraft was interned in Romania.

After the delivery of the Douglas DC-2 aircraft, the Polish Ministry of Transport instructed PZL to create designs for an airliner based on this American model, a decision that made it out of date before it was even drawn up. It was to have accommodation for 14 passengers. The aircraft was powered by two Wright Cyclones and was envisaged as a replacement for LOT's Fokker F.VIIb/3ms. The type that emerged, the PZL.44 Wicher (Gale), was smaller and heavier than the DC-2; it also had a lower cruising speed than the DC-2, but a slightly greater range. The Wicher first flew in March 1938, and it went to LOT for trials, which lasted until March 1939. The aircraft was used on the routes from Warsaw to Lwów and from Warsaw to Gdynia, but it showed some shortcomings and did not meet its estimated performance. As LOT was not overenthusiastic about Polish-designed aircraft – an attitude that led to much friction between the airline and the government department responsible for aviation – the Wicher was returned to its manufacturer. While the Wicher was being designed, LOT had already decided to buy a series of American-built Lockheed Model 10 Electras in 1936. Four aircraft arrived by ship at the port of Gdynia the same year. They were assembled at Rumia Airport and subsequently flown to Warsaw. In 1937, the remaining aircraft arrived. That year, it was decided to buy also the new, enlarged version: the Lockheed Model 14 Super Electras. The first of these aircraft arrived in April and May 1938. The managers of LOT decided to use the purchase of these modern aircraft for propaganda purposes. The last aircraft, bought in Burbank, would be flown to Warsaw. It was to be a test in the possible launch of an airline connecting Warsaw with New York and Chicago. The flight took place in May 1938. The crew consisted of Wacław Makowski (LOT director and first pilot), Zbigniew Wysiekierski (co-pilot), Szymon Piskorz (mechanic), Alfons Rzeczewski (radio navigator) and Jerzy Krassowski (assistant). Flying via Mazatlán (Mexico), Guatemala, Lima, Buenos Aires and Rio de Janeiro, the aircraft reached Natal in Brazil. From there, in 11 hours and 10 minutes, the crew crossed the Atlantic Ocean and landed in Dakar. The route led through Senegal, Casablanca, Tunis and Rome, finally arriving in Warsaw.

In the meantime, LOT had sent all of its Junkers F 13 aircraft back to the Junkers factory in exchange for a single Ju 52 aircraft, which would be used on the Warsaw–Berlin and Warsaw–Thessaloniki routes. Unfortunately, Polish people would soon see more aircraft of this type when German forces invaded Poland in 1939. During the war, the LOT Ju 52 escaped to Bucharest, where the aircraft was seized by the Romanian government. During the invasion, German forces destroyed the Warsaw airport, its buildings and hangars. The German invasion also resulted in the end of the Free City of Danzig, which was occupied and became a base for the Luftwaffe.

When LOT was set up as a national airline under government control, the Junkers F 13 remained in service. Some were equipped with skis for operations in wintertime. (National Digital Archive Poland)

LOT obtained a series of Fokker F.VII three-engined aircraft, which were built under licence in Poland. (National Digital Archive Poland)

This Fokker F.VII three-engined passenger aircraft was used on the Warsaw to Bucharest route and was equipped with skis for operations in wintertime. (National Digital Archive Poland)

Left: Two LOT Fokker F.VII's in LOT's hangar at Warsaw Mokotow Airport. (National Digital Archive Poland)

Below: LOT evaluated the Polish-built Lublin R-XVI as a possible replacement for the Junkers F 13, but the aircraft did not satisfy the needs of the airline. It went into service as an ambulance plane instead. (National Digital Archive Poland)

The PZl.4, although evaluated by LOT, was found to be unsatisfactory for the airline. (National Digital Archive Poland)

Above: This PWS-24 was used on the route between Warsaw and Poznań. (National Digital Archive Poland)

Right: LOT bought a small number of PWS-24 aircraft, like this one that was used on the Warsaw to Poznań route. (National Digital Archive Poland)

Below: In 1935, LOT decided to buy three Douglas DC-2 aircraft. (National Digital Archive Poland)

This Douglas DC-2 was built by Fokker and served on LOT international routes until it was interned in Riga during the war. (National Digital Archive Poland)

The Douglas DC-2 also transported Polish mail. (National Digital Archive Poland)

The PZL.44 Wicher was evaluated by LOT on routes from Warsaw to Lwów and Gdynia, but it was not bought by the airline. (National Digital Archive Poland)

LOT exchanged its old Junkers F 13s for one single Ju 52, seen here in front of a British Airways Lockheed Super Electra. (National Digital Archive Poland)

Above: Lockheed Model 10 Electras joined the fleet in 1936. (National Digital Archive Poland)

Left: This Lockheed Model 10 Electra would crash on a flight from Warsaw via Bucharest to Athens in 1936. (National Digital Archive Poland)

Below: The Lockheed Electra was used on international routes and served LOT's propaganda purposes. (National Digital Archive Poland)

Right: The cockpit of a Lockheed Model 10 Electra. (National Digital Archive Poland)

Below: The Lockheed Model 14 Super Electra was ordered in 1937. (National Digital Archive Poland).

A Lockheed Model 14 Super Electra is seen in Lima while on a delivery flight. (National Digital Archive Poland).

Chapter 3
Post-war Reorganisation

Wen, in 1944, Russian troops started the 'liberation' of Poland, a new occupation started. The powers of the Kremlin were exercised in Poland with the help of the Polish Workers' Party. To preserve the appearance of democracy, pre-war institutions were revived, but they would now take place under communist leadership. LOT had lost its entire fleet, through both wartime destruction and confiscation by enemy troops. The company management was replaced by military directors who were members of the communist party. The only remainder of pre-war LOT was the crane, the company's logo.

The origins of post-war LOT can be found with the Civil Aviation Department, which was organised in 1944. The department decided to launch two circular flight routes; one route was between Lublin and Białystok, whereas the other was routed from Lublin via Przemyśl and Rzeszów back to Lublin. Additionally, a flight to Minsk was launched, but this destination was replaced with Warsaw after 17 January 1945. Flights to Lwów and Vilnius were considered, but Moscow banned them because these cities were now part of the Soviet Union, and they wished to operate flights with Aeroflot rather than LOT. The flights were carried out for the Polski Komitet Wyzwolenia Narodowego (PKWN, Polish Committee of National Liberation), which was a communist provisional entity, backed by Soviets, working in opposition to the Western-backed Polish government-in-exile. As LOT had lost all its aircraft during the war, three Lisunov Li-2 aircraft were used. Most of the passengers on these ad hoc flights were functionaries of the new government or the communist party. Later on, small Polikarpov PO-2 biplanes were also introduced to transport mail, service mail and propaganda materials.[1]

On 6 March 1945, LOT Polish Airlines was officially reactivated by the Civil Aviation Department. A few days later, it was decided that the Air Force Command would take care of the reorganisation of the airline. To this end, several new aviation units within the air force were created. The 7th Independent Civil Aviation Transport Squadron – with a fleet of ten Li-2 aircraft – was one of them, and it would carry out passenger flights. The 18th and 19th Independent Civil Aviation Regiments – with a fleet of more than 100 Polikarpov PO-2 aircraft – would guarantee delivery of mail and newspapers as well as propaganda materials. The 8th Independent Transport Squadron would perform flights commissioned by the Ministry of Public Security.[2]

On 30 March 1945, the 7th Independent Civil Aviation Transport Squadron – which took over the task of performing pre-war LOT Polish Airlines duties – decided to start up the first circular route from Warsaw via Łódź, Kraków, Rzeszów, Lublin and back to Warsaw. During the first three months of operation, about 1,500 flights were made with 20,000 passengers. In March, April and May 1945, regional branches of LOT were established in several Polish cities. The establishment of such branches was in line with the policies of the Soviet managers of Aeroflot, who were also setting up regional branches for the airline in several Russian cities. This situation would last until 18 July 1945, when the Council of Ministers decided to re-establish LOT Polish Airlines as a state enterprise. Polish pilots were hired to replace the Russian pilots who had previously operated the flights. On 6 December 1945, the civil aviation transport units that had been set up by the air force were dismantled, and all Lisunov aircraft were transferred to the airline. They were painted in LOT's colours and registered in Poland. The Polikarpov aircraft, on the other hand, went to the Department of Civil Aviation. However, this new setup of the airline did not guarantee managerial freedoms for its managers. The Polish communist party, which remained a strong power within the country, continued to demand a large number of flights to transport party members and propaganda materials. As a result, the new airline could only operate a limited number of 150 commercial flights between September and December 1945.[3]

With its fleet of Lisunov aircraft – which were Russian-made copies of the Douglas DC-3 Dakota – LOT started up the first regular connection between Warsaw and Gdańsk. The aircraft proved to be very efficient and would remain in service until 1969 (by which time the airline had used a total of 40 Lisunovs). Besides the Russian 'copy', LOT also purchased the original DC-3. In 1946, an order for nine of these aircraft was signed. The type was readily available from war surplus, so they were very cheap. Originally, the aircraft had been fitted with metal benches in the cabins, but LOT modernised the cabins, placing 21 seats in a 2+1 arrangement. Later on, in 1957, the cabins were once again refitted, now with 24 seats. The American aircraft were used on international services to Paris, Stockholm, Prague and Berlin. The last DC-3 in LOT-service entered the fleet in 1959 and was sold to Iran when it was retired.

In order to further expand its international route network, LOT was also looking into the possibilities of obtaining larger aircraft, preferably with four engines. On 21 March 1947, a French SNCASE SE-161 Languedoc was demonstrated in Warsaw. Although it was LOT's intention to buy up to ten of these aircraft, the first order (signed in May 1947) was for only five. The first of these aircraft entered commercial service on 1 August 1947. However, LOT was not satisfied with their performance, specifically when it came to the engines, which often caused problems. On 31 May 1948, one of these aircraft (SP-LDA) developed engine problems on a flight between Warsaw and Paris. Three of the four engines stopped working, and the aircraft forcibly landed with folded landing gear near Reims. Fortunately, there were no fatalities. Although the manufacturer offered to replace the engines with Pratt & Whitney R-1830s, LOT decided to retire the model. Of course, the problems with this aircraft type, which had been manufactured in the West, gave rise to a series of disputes with the Polish Workers' Party. The authorities of the Polish People's Republic (established in 1947) accused several LOT managers related to the operation of the Languedoc of sabotage activities and corruption. Several of them were sentenced to death.[4] In the meantime, the international route map had been extended, with routes to Bucharest, Budapest, Belgrade and Copenhagen.

The post-war LOT would use a total of 40 Lisunov Li-2s from 1945 until 1969. (National Digital Archive Poland).

Above: The Lisunov Li-2 was a Soviet-built copy of the American Douglas DC-3. (LOT Polish Airlines)

Left: The Polikarpov PO-2 served to deliver mail and propaganda materials. (Michel Derela/Wikimedia Commons Licence)

Below left: LOT ordered a total of five Languedoc aircraft, but they were soon retired, as they developed engine problems. (LOT Polish Airlines)

Below right: A LOT Douglas DC-3 Dakota, ready for the inaugural flight to Brussels. (LOT Polish Airlines)

Chapter 4
Fleet Modernisation

The problems with the French Languedoc airliners gave a reason to Soviet-aligned managers at LOT to buy Russian-made aircraft. In 1949, the airline bought five Ilyushin Il-12B passenger aircraft with a seating capacity of 18–21 passengers. A sixth aircraft was rented for a few months in 1952. These aircraft would remain in service until 1957, and three of them were even kept in reserve until November 1959. As a result, LOT could increase its network by adding Bucharest, Budapest, Brussels and Copenhagen.

In 1955, LOT decided to buy four Ilyushin Il-14 aircraft: a further development of the IL-12. As the Il-12 had shown problems with the engines, the Il-14 was designed with new engines and nacelles, which solved these problems. The Il-14 was intended as a replacement for the DC-3 and the Li-2. In 1956, LOT bought two more Il-14s from the Soviet Union, but also ordered six VEB Il-14 aircraft (licence-built Il-14s, made in East Germany), as well as one AV-14 with large loading doors. The AV-14 was built under licence in Czechoslovakia and was designed as a passenger aircraft with large cargo capacity. While the Il-14 was in service, the aircraft underwent different modernisations. The number of seats was increased from 18 to 26 and – on some aircraft – even to 32. With its new fleet, LOT could further expand its network to include Vienna and Moscow. It may be a surprise to many that communist-ruled Poland only started up flights to Moscow in 1955, but one should keep in mind that passenger flights between Poland and Russia had previously been operated by military aircraft. Thanks to the expansion of its network, LOT recorded more than one million passengers in 1955: the first time this magical number was reached.[1]

Whereas Poland was essentially forced to buy aircraft built behind the Iron Curtain, Western countries were not eager to accept such aircraft in their airspace. Some took administrative measures that made it difficult for LOT to fly there with its Russian-made fleet, while other Western countries banned the LOT aircraft completely. However, one should also remember that the Il-14 lacked the sophistication of Western aircraft, and Western passengers were also not at all eager to fly on Russian-made aircraft. When the Belgian airline Sabena decided to sell off some Convair Liner CV-240 aircraft, LOT grabbed the opportunity to buy three of these second-hand aircraft, which were powered by Pratt & Whitney R-2800-CB16 engines. In April 1958, the Convairs entered commercial service and could be seen on flights from Warsaw–Vienna, Warsaw–Paris, Warsaw–London and Warsaw–Zürich routes. As the aircraft performed well, LOT managed to buy another second-hand Convair from KLM and one more from Iran Air.

Although previous attempts to build Polish aircraft for LOT were far from successful, in 1956, PZL Okęcie made another attempt at designing an aircraft for the Polish airline. Originally, it was the intention to use two Soviet Shvetsov Ash-21 engines to power the PZL.12, but as production ceased, the aircraft was redesigned with four Polish WN-3 engines. The first prototype of the new aircraft – intended to replace the Il-14 – made its maiden flight on 21 July 1959. A second prototype, this time with a complete passenger cabin, made its first flight on 7 January 1961. One of the prototypes was evaluated by LOT in August–September 1961 on the Warsaw–Rzeszów route, carrying over 1,700 passengers. It was also used in 1961 and 1962 on the Warsaw–Poznań route. Although the PZL.12 proved easier to fly than the Il-14, LOT found it unprofitable to order additional aircraft for domestic routes.[2]

In March 1961, LOT received its first three Ilyushin Il-18 aircraft, followed by a fourth one in April 1964. With these larger aircraft, the airline could expand its route network. First, the new type would be introduced on the Warsaw–Moscow route, but soon Polish Il-18s would show up in many European countries. The aircraft offered several advantages. It had a large capacity (87 seats in Lux class, later changed to 99 seats in Economy and still later to 105 seats). It is odd to notice that the first aircraft, introduced on the Warsaw–Moscow route, only offered Lux-class, comparable to today's business class, yet most passengers were members of the communist party. The cabin of the aircraft was very spacious, with wide comfortable seats and a lot of legroom. However, the Il-18 was very noisy, and passengers experienced heavy vibrations from the engines. Nevertheless, LOT would keep these aircraft in service until the 1990s, when they were sold to Polonia Airways. Two Il-18s had been converted to freighters in the meantime. LOT used a total of nine IL-18s, which were used to expand the network to Baghdad, Beirut, Benghazi, Damascus and Tunis.

Although LOT had made serious efforts to modernise its fleet, it still mainly comprised Russian-built aircraft. The airline operated outdated Lisunov Li-2s and Douglas DC-3s alongside Russian-built Il-12s, Il-14s and Il-18s. When the airline intended to further expand its footprint by starting up flights to Rome, Amsterdam and Cairo, the managers were convinced Western markets needed more modern Western aircraft. The Russian-built LOT fleet did not offer the level of comfort needed to attract Western passengers. At first, a LOT committee studied the possibilities of buying new aircraft, but it was clear these would have to be paid for in hard currency: something Poland could not afford. When British United Airlines (BUA) decided to sell three Viscount Type 804 aircraft, this was a great opportunity for LOT to obtain Western aircraft at a relatively lower price. The British aircraft were five years old and had mainly served on domestic routes in the British Isles. They offered room for 56 passengers, and their cruising speed was twice that of the Il-12/14. However, the British aircraft would be sold to Poland without their radar equipment. The reasons behind this decision are not very clear. Some sources state that, by removing the radars from the three aircraft, the purchase price could be further reduced. Other authors indicate that BUA was not allowed to sell aircraft with a radar to a communist country, as these systems could be used for military purposes. According to some Russian sources, the British radars were considered to be obsolete and had to be replaced by Russian-made systems anyway.

Of course, Polish pilots had to be trained to fly the British-made Viscounts. In September 1962, a group of 15 experienced pilots left for England. They passed the theoretical part of the training without any problems. Flying the aircraft, however, became an interesting experience. In the UK, ILS (Instrument Landing System) operations had been introduced and had become standard practice. However, in Poland, pilots were still used to flying with visual references or the NDB (non-directional beacon) system. British instructors were therefore amazed to notice how well the Polish pilots managed to fly the Viscounts. After eight weeks of training, LOT decided the pilots had received enough training and called them back to their home country, although the British instructors insisted further training would be useful. Of course, there were different reasons for this Polish decision. First of all, keeping a team of 15 people overseas for a long time would turn out to be expensive, but above all, LOT feared its pilots would like the Western habits and comfort so much, they would not want to return. Upon their return, it was decided the Viscounts would be flown with a crew of three (instead of two as was normal with other airlines). The third person in the cockpit would have to be a trusted member of the communist party, in order to avoid pilots flying the Viscounts to the West to ask for asylum. The first Viscount was delivered to LOT on 6 November 1962, with the second following on 27 November, and the third one on 22 December. However, the Viscounts would not serve for a long time. Two of them were lost in crashes: the first on 19 December 1962, after it had only flown 84 hours in LOT service. A second Viscount crashed on 20 August 1965. After these accidents, LOT decided to get rid of the third remaining aircraft. It made its last scheduled flight in 1966, after which it was sold to New Zealand.[3]

Above: Following the problems with the French Languadoc aircraft, Russia offered the Il-12. (Jozef Mols collection)

Right: With the Il-14, LOT could expand its network to also include Amsterdam. (Thijs Postma)

Below: For a while, the Il-14 became the backbone of the LOT fleet. (Thijs Postma)

Above: When Sabena sold its Convair 240s, it was a good occasion for LOT to obtain three of them. (LOT Polish Airlines)

Left: When the Polish MD-12 was built, the factory made the single prototype available to LOT for evaluation, but the model was never built in series. (Jozef Mols collection)

Below: LOT received its first Il-18 aircraft in March 1961. (National Digital Archive Poland)

Above: LOT would use a total of nine
Ilyushin Il-18s. (National Digital Archive
Poland)

Right: This Ilyushin Il-18 is being prepared
for its next flight. (National Digital
Archive Poland)

Below: LOT obtained three Viscount 800s
from British United Airlines. (LOT Polish
Airlines)

Chapter 5
The Jet Age

As the Il-12 and Il-14 aircraft, as well as the remaining Li-2s, became obsolete, LOT adopted the twin-engined Antonov An-24 turboprop. The aircraft delivered excellent services until the beginning of the 1990s when they were replaced by ATR equipment. Nevertheless, the operation of the Russian-built aircraft was not without problems, and three of the An-24s crashed. The most tragic accident occurred on 23 April 1969, when an aircraft crashed in the Babia Góra mountain range, killing all 53 people on board.

Like many other airlines in Europe, LOT was considering purchasing jet aircraft. It was clear the airline would have to buy Russian-built airliners, so the Tupolev Tu-134 became the obvious choice. The budget for 1968 included the purchase of five of these aircraft. The aircraft was of the first export version and had a glass nose. Two aircraft arrived on 6 November 1968: the first of these would be decommissioned in June 1982 and sold to Aeroflot; the second was damaged beyond repair during a landing incident on 23 January 1980. Three more Tu-134s arrived in April and May 1969. They served until June 1982, when they were also sold to Aeroflot.

As LOT was pleased with the introduction of its first jets, a decision was made in 1972 to purchase more of these aircraft, this time in the 'A' variant. These aircraft offered room for 84 passengers thanks to the extension of the fuselage by 83in (2.1m). Externally, they did not differ that much from the older version, except for the fact that the 'A' version had a larger horizontal tail. The avionics had also been upgraded. The first three of these aircraft arrived in March and April 1973. When the aircraft were retired from service, one was scrapped in 1993. A second one was handed over to the Polish Aviation Museum in Kraków in 1997. The third one was set up in Warsaw as a police training object, used to train anti-terrorist police units. In 1976, LOT would receive a further two Tu-134s, which would serve until 1994. With the new jet equipment, LOT could launch new routes to Kyiv and Istanbul. From 1969 onwards, the LOT jets operated from the new Okęcie Airport in Warsaw.

The 1970s witnessed great changes in the political system in Poland. Władysław Gomułka had been the de facto leader of post-war Poland from 1947 until 1948. From 1956 to 1970, following political unrest, he once again became the leader of the country. He was initially very popular for his reforms, seeking a 'Polish way to socialism'. During the 1960s, however, he became more rigid and authoritarian, and he was not inclined to introduce or permit changes. Using anti-Zionist political propaganda, he managed to turn away attention from the stagnating economy. He was also responsible for persecuting protesting students and toughening censorship on the media. Economic difficulties in 1970 led to price rises and subsequent bloody clashes with shipyard workers on the Baltic coast. These tragic events forced Gomułka's resignation.[1] In December 1970, Edward Gierek was appointed as First Secretary and de facto leader of the Polish People's Republic. The first years of his term were marked by industrialisation and the improvement of living and working conditions. He had spent time in Western Europe (he was member of the Belgian Resistance during World War Two), and so he opened communist Poland to new Western ideas and loosened the censorship, thus turning Poland into the most liberal country of the Eastern Bloc.[2] With World War Two nearly 25 years in the past, Polish people who had emigrated prior to the world conflict or as a result of the war, wanted to come to Poland more often to visit their relatives. Polish citizens were also seeking opportunities to visit their relatives abroad. In order to respond to this desire, Gierek authorised LOT to start up its first intercontinental flights across the Atlantic. Of course, offers from Boeing (707) and Douglas (DC-8) were unacceptable to the Polish government, which – notwithstanding a more relaxed policy – still had strong ties with the Soviet Union. Therefore, the airline had to buy Ilyushin Il-62 four-engined jets. In March 1972, the first of these aircraft was delivered. LOT would use a total of seven Il-62s. Of course, crews for the new aircraft had to be trained. The training was performed at the Sheremetyevo Airport near Moscow. On 16 April 1973, an Il-62 took off from Warsaw to New York with a full passenger cabin. Earlier, an Il-62 was used on charter flights to Toronto, inaugurating the first transatlantic route in LOT's history. Later, the aircraft type would also be used to start up routes to the Far East. Bangkok was served with stops in Dubai and Mumbai. The Il-62 could also be seen on routes to Kuwait, Tripoli and Algiers. Charter flights to Sydney and Tokyo were also operated by Il-62s.

As LOT was expanding – and simultaneously becoming more open to the West – it was time to introduce a new livery design for the aircraft. Roman Duszek and Andrzej Zbrożek developed the new design: the fuselage was painted in white with a large italic title 'LOT' on the front; the crane, the enduring symbol of LOT, remained on the tail, together with the Polish flag. The introduction of the new design coincided with LOT's 50th anniversary in 1979.

Optimism about the success of the Il-62 would soon disappear, however, when, on 14 March 1980, LOT Flight 007 from New York City to Warsaw crashed during an attempt to land at Okęcie Airport, killing all 77 passengers and 10 crew members. According to investigators, metal fatigue in a turbine disc may have caused the accident, and Poland blamed the Russian technicians for their sloppy overhaul of the engines. As a result, all Il-62 aircraft were replaced with Il-62Ms – LOT modernised some of its IL-62s to IL-62M standard, while other aircraft were exchanged for the newer version. This decision would be of very little help, however. On 9 May 1987, another Il-62 (this time the 'M' variant) crashed, and, once again, the cause was improper engine overhaul.

There were more dark clouds on the Polish horizon. The Polish leader, Edward Gierek, had financed industrialisation, the building of social housing flats, education and modern health services mainly by using foreign loans. However, most of the funds, lent by foreign creditors, were directed at constructing blocks of flats and at creating heavy steel and coal industries in his native Silesia, more than any other part of the country. The country was so heavily indebted to its creditors that rationing was introduced when the government became unable to pay off the loans. In 1980, Gierek allowed the establishment of the Solidarity Trade Union in Gdańsk; this was the first trade union in Poland which was not controlled by the communist party. As such, this was seen as a radical move to renounce communism and Gierek was removed from office.[3] Despite dragging Poland into financial and economic decline, Gierek is fondly remembered for his patriotism and modernisation policies.

After Gierek left Poland severely indebted, General Wojciech Jaruzelski became head of state. As Poland headed towards insolvency, rationing was increased owing to shortages of basic goods, which only contributed to the tense social and political situation. The declining living conditions triggered anger among the masses and strengthened anti-communist sentiment. The Solidarity Movement was also gaining support, worrying not only the Polish Central Committee but also the Soviet Union, which viewed Solidarity as a threat to the Warsaw Pact. Fearing a Soviet intervention similar to those in Hungary and Czechoslovakia, Jaruzelski chose to impose martial law in Poland on 13 December 1981 in order to crush the anti-communist opposition. A military junta – the first such junta in a communist country – imposed a curfew and travel restrictions that would last until 22 July 1983.[4] Due to the introduction of martial law, all LOT flights were suspended, and foreign aircraft were not admitted to Poland. In the spring of 1982, LOT could restart domestic flights, but there were few passengers. In order to obtain a ticket, people had to apply for a special authorisation from the political authorities. On all flights, there were at least two armed officers of the Polish Secret Service on board.

In 1983, LOT could resume its European flights, but it would only be on 28 April 1984 that flights to New York and Chicago resumed. That year, new routes to New Delhi and Beijing were also launched. The 1980s also saw the economic situation in all eastern European countries getting worse. For LOT, it was more and more difficult to keep the exhausted fleet of Il-18s and Tu-134s in full working order. To save the situation, the airline obtained some Yakovlev Yak-40 jets on loan from the 36th Special Regiment of Transport Aviation. In the meantime, LOT had also received the An-12 cargo aircraft from the Polish Air Force.

Above: Antonov An-24s replaced obsolete IL-12 and Il-14 aircraft. (National Digital Archive Poland)

Left: The Antonov An-24 was mainly used on domestic services. (National Digital Archive Poland)

LOT entered the jet age with the introduction of the Tupolev Tu-134. (National Digital Archive Poland).

The Tupolev Tu-134 – seen here at Helsinki Airport – was used on European routes. (Helsinki City Museum).

Above: A LOT Tupolev Tu-134 at a Swiss airport. (ETH Bibliothek Zürich)

Right: With the Ilyushin Il-62, LOT was able to offer transatlantic services. (National Digital Archive Poland)

Above: Baptism of a new Il-62M. (National Digital Archive Poland)

Left: Passengers boarding an Il-62 for a transatlantic flight. (National Digital Archive Poland)

Below: A LOT Ilyushin IL-62M in flight. (Clipperarctic/CC BY-SA 2.0 via Wikimedia Commons)

This Aeroflot Ilyushin Il-62 was chartered by LOT to supplement the fleet. (National Digital Archive Poland)

LOT received some Yakovlev YAK-40 jets on loan from the Polish Air Force. (National Digital Archives Poland)

The Yak-40 was used by LOT on both domestic and regional routes. (Jozef Mols)

LOT also used Antonov An-12 aircraft in the cargo role. (Udo Haafke GFDL 1.2 via Wikimedia Commons)

Chapter 6
Western Aircraft

Somewhere around the middle of the 1980s, Jaruzelski realised that – after the period of martial law – it was necessary to re-liberalise Polish society. Political prisoners received amnesty and he reinstated a multi-party political system. It became clear, however, that he had lost his authority, and his influence did not reach much further than the outskirts of Warsaw; in the rest of the country, the government had lost its grip. Owing to the political crisis, martial law, and the resulting collapse of commercial air traffic in Poland, LOT also suffered. It became clear that it was time to withdraw the Il-18 and Tu-134 aircraft from commercial service as, during the crisis, maintenance of these aircraft had been below standard. To replace the outdated aircraft, Tupolev Tu-154M aircraft were ordered; however, Tu-154B aircraft were delivered as the 'M' variants were not ready.

In May 1985, two Tu-154B-2 aircraft arrived in Warsaw, and a third one arrived in May 1986. The aircraft were given the colours of LOT, but the registrations were Russian. These three aircraft were 'on loan' and had room for 164 passengers. They would fly until 1988, when they were replaced by more modern 'M' variants. The first purchased TU-154M with 150 seats arrived in Poland in May 1986. During the first days of its operation, LOT staff made numerous comments about ways to improve its safety and comfort, and, by the time the fourth 'M' aircraft arrived in August 1987, many changes had been made. First of all, all inscriptions on the aircraft, including the flight deck, were in Polish rather than Russian to help increase safety. The passenger cabin had a 150-seat configuration, with 52 seats in a front cabin of a higher standard (but not comparable to today's business class). In the second cabin, there was room for 98 seats. In this 'tourist' class, leg room was reduced. Instructions regarding the safety on board were clear, and the aircraft had also received a new evacuation system in the form of six inflatable slides. In order to increase passenger comfort, the galley had been changed and enlarged. Thanks to new buffets, catering on board was much more efficient with the introduction of ten carts (instead of only two in the previous B-2 version of the aircraft). Pilots could enjoy the new long-distance navigation system consisting of two Omega-sets, linked to the automatic pilot. The introduction of the Tu-154 was indeed a great step forwards for LOT, both in terms of safety and passenger comfort. The aircraft would end scheduled services in 1993 and continue to fly occasional charter flights until 1996. Near the same time the Tu-154s entered service, LOT also obtained some Antonov An-26 aircraft on loan from the Polish Air Force, in order to augment the cargo capacity of the airline.

In the meantime, LOT management had to solve other problems as well. After the crash of Flight 5055 on 9 May 1987, bound from Warsaw to New York and operated by an Il-62M, the American Federal Aviation Administration issued a ban on the entry of Il-62 aircraft to the US. On the one hand, the transatlantic routes were very important for Polish people wishing to visit relatives on the other side of the ocean. On the other hand, the Ilyushin Il-62 was the only aircraft type in LOT's fleet capable of crossing the Atlantic. Therefore, a single Douglas DC-8 Super 62 was leased from International Air Leases, and operated by Arrow Air Inc, which provided the crews and flew under certificate on behalf of LOT. Two mechanics were seconded to Warsaw to oversee maintenance. Additionally, a spare parts package was included in the lease contract. The aircraft was flown by American pilots, and the cabin crew included both Polish and American members. With the DC-8, LOT operated services to New York, but it was also planned to add flights to Chicago and Detroit. The aircraft remained with LOT until August 1988 and was the first Western-built aircraft in its fleet.

Of course, the introduction of the DC-8 had only been an ad hoc decision in order to continue flights to the US. It was very clear that LOT needed new aircraft of its own, able to fly the transatlantic route and possibly other long-distance flights. In 1988, the Polish authorities decided to buy Boeing 767 aircraft for LOT, however, at first, three aircraft would be leased for up to 20 years. Thanks to this leasing, there was no burden on the state budget as it was financed by annual income in foreign currency, earned by LOT from the transatlantic flights. The first two aircraft were 767-200ERs with a seating capacity of 208 passengers, of which 18 were in business class and 190 were in economy class. They were delivered in April and May 1989, respectively. The aircraft had a range of 12,000km (6,475nm), and this made it possible to start up a long-distance flight from Warsaw to Singapore. The third aircraft was a Boeing 767-300ER. This aircraft had a longer fuselage, and therefore could take up to 249 passengers (24 in business class and 225 in economy class). The aircraft arrived in Warsaw in June 1990. With the introduction of the 767, LOT became one of the first carriers in Central and Eastern Europe to use American equipment. However, the three 767s in the fleet were not enough to cover demand during the summer months. So, LOT decided to obtain another 767-200ER on short-term lease from Air New Zealand. This aircraft was used in the summers of 1992, 1993 and 1994. At the same time, a Douglas DC-10-30 was leased from Finnair from 21 February 1994 until 26 March 1994, as well as two other aircraft of the same type obtained from Malaysian Airlines. When, in May 1995, LOT received its own fourth 767-300ER, it was no longer necessary to lease the aircraft from Air New Zealand. In 1996, LOT once again rented another 767-300ER, this time from Gulf Air, in order to cope with increasing demand until delivery of LOT's own fifth 767-300ER, which arrived in May 1997.

In the meantime, the political scene in the Eastern Bloc countries had changed dramatically. The Berlin Wall had come down in 1989, and revolutions in Central and Eastern Europe also influenced Poland. Jaruzelski supported the change of government for the benefit of the country and resigned, which led to multi-party elections in Poland. He would briefly serve as president of Poland, but he exercised no real power; in the 1990 Polish election, Lech Wałęsa succeeded him as the first president elected in a popular vote. Poland entered the Western world and had to adapt to capitalist principles. This was also the case for LOT Polish Airlines, which saw an enormous increase in demand as Polish citizens could now travel without restrictions. Both demand for long-distance travel and flights to holiday destinations grew. In 1994, LOT signed a codeshare agreement with American Airlines on flights to and from Warsaw, as well as onward flights in the US and Poland, operated by both companies.

LOT's acquisition of the long-range Boeing 767 airliners enabled the company to reposition itself as a transit airline, offering flights between European cities – via Warsaw – to selected long-distance destinations. This coincided with the growing demand for long-range travel, noticed in several Eastern European countries.

This Tupolev Tu-154 was delivered to LOT in 1987. (Jozef Mols)

Above: The Tupolev Tu-154M replaced the outdated Il-18s and Tu-134s. (Jozef Mols)

Right: This Antonov An-26 was operated by the Polish Air Force but joined the LOT fleet as a cargo plane for a few months in 1991. (Jozef Mols)

Below: A LOT Antonov An-26 cargo plane at Manchester Airport. (Ken Fielding/https://www.flickr.com/photos/kenfielding, CC BY-SA 3.0 via Wikimedia Commons Licence)

Left: LOT had to lease this Douglas DC-8 in order to continue its transatlantic flights. (Clinton Groves GFDL 1.2 via Wikimedia Commons)

Below: With the Boeing 767-200, LOT could continue its transatlantic flights. (Aero Icarus Zurich/CC BY-SA 2.0 Wikimedia Commons Licence)

The first three Boeing 767-200s were leased. (BriYYZ/CC BY-SA 2.0 Wikimedia Commons Licence)

Above left: A LOT Boeing 767-300ER is seen at Singapore Airport. (National Digital Archive Poland)

Above right: A Boeing 767-300ER is seen at Manchester Airport. (Ken Fielding/https://www.flickr.com/photos/kenfielding, CC BY-SA 3.0 via Wikimedia Commons Licence)

Right: A Boeing 767-300ER is seen at Poznań Airport. (Azymut [Rafał M. Socha] at pl.wikipedia, CC BY-SA 3.0 via Wikimedia Commons)

Below: While waiting for the delivery of its Boeing 767-300ERs, LOT had to lease DC-10-30s like this one from Malaysian Airlines. (Jozef Mols collection)

Chapter 7

The Regional Fleet

Of course, expanding the international network and modernising the long-haul fleet was of utmost importance for LOT after the fall of the Berlin Wall and the subsequent increased demand for holidays abroad. The demand was not limited to transatlantic routes. Polish people also wanted to travel to European destinations, and in order to feed LOT international flights, outdated regional aircraft had to be replaced. Therefore, LOT was looking for a successor of the Antonov An-24, which had been heavily utilised on domestic and regional routes. As a result of negotiations with several manufacturers, LOT decided to order eight ATR 72-200 aircraft with an option for two more. First delivery was planned for June 1991, although the aircraft, SP-LFA, actually arrived in Poland on 15 August 1991. Part of the contract included a barter agreement. Polish manufacturer PZL Mielec would produce aviation components for French aircraft manufacturers, and the value of these components would be deducted from the invoice for the ATRs.[1]

When the first ATRs entered the fleet, their use was not limited to domestic services, and they were also used on routes to Vilnius (Lithuania), Kyiv (Ukraine), Minsk (Belarus) and Lviv (Ukraine). The aircraft performed very well during their service. Only one had to be written off after it crashed into an airport tractor while taxiing; thankfully, this incident happened without injury to the passengers.

In order to handle the increasing number of passengers, a new terminal building was officially opened in the early 1990s at the Warsaw-Okęcie Airport, capable of handling five million passengers per year. A few years later, however, the terminal already turned out to be too small.[2] LOT itself had to adapt its business practices to the new market economy. Therefore, the holding company of the airline (PLL LOT) was transformed into a single-shareholder company of the Polish State Treasury. Furthermore, in line with practices of other European airlines, LOT introduced its Voyager Loyalty Program for passengers who frequently travelled with the airline.

Besides the replacement of the AN-24 by ATRs, LOT was also interested in obtaining modern Western jet aircraft to be used on regional routes. After the successful debut of the Boeing 767 in 1991, the airline decided to obtain a fleet of Boeing 737 Classic aircraft. For starters, the airline ordered four 737-400s and five 737-500s, with delivery of the first aircraft planned for the second half of 1992. While LOT waited for the delivery of these aircraft, a 737-500 (SE-DNI) was leased from Lingeflyg from Sweden. It would remain in service until March 1993. A second, identical aircraft, also from Lingeflyg, was leased between May 1992 and April 1993. In December 1992, the airline received its first own 737-500 (SP-LKA). A few days later, SP-LKB arrived in Poland. Before the end of the year, two more copies arrived. The first 737-400, SP-LLA, arrived in April 1993. With the delivery of the new aircraft, the leased 737-500s could be returned. In June, a second '400' was received, and the fifth aircraft (a 737-45D) arrived at the same time. With the introduction of the jets, LOT opened routes from Warsaw via Stockholm to Oslo and to Riga, alongside a route from Katowice to Frankfurt and one from Wrocław via Poznań to Düsseldorf. In 1995, routes from Gdańsk to Copenhagen and from Kraków to Zürich were added. In the 1994 IATA report, the LOT fleet was considered to be amongst the youngest of all airlines in the world, thanks to the purchase of Boeing 767s, ATRs and Boeing 737s.[3] In 1996, LOT took delivery of a used 737-300 (SP-LMB) that had previously served with Air Europa, Iberia and Aviatec. This aircraft would remain in service until August 1997, when more 737-400s were delivered directly from the factory.

In 1996, as LOT wanted to concentrate its activities around the ever growing regional and intercontinental operations, the airline decided to set up a subsidiary to handle domestic air traffic under the brand name Eurolot. The company was to function as a low-cost airline. Regular air operations started on 1 July 1997. To start up operations, the new airline leased a fleet of eight ATR 72 aircraft from LOT, later to be joined by two more ATR 72s and 13 ATR 42s. Additionally, crews were delivered by LOT. Between 1998 and 2000, Eurolot would also use two BAE Jetstream 31 aircraft. The primary task of Eurolot was to reduce operational costs on domestic and regional flights, previously operated by LOT. In the following years, the smaller ATR 42-300 was purchased for Eurolot. A total of five second-hand aircraft were added to the fleet and would serve until 2006.[4]

After the purchase of ATR turboprops and Boeing jets, LOT was also interested in the purchase of smaller jet aircraft. The Brazilian Embraer ERJ145 was a good choice because of the short order completion time, favourable cost-effect system and better technical parameters in comparison to the ATRs. In 1999, a contract was signed regarding the purchase of six of these Brazilian jets, with an option for another six. The first ERJ145 (SP-LGA) reached Poland in July 1999. It made its first commercial flight on 1 August 1999 on the Warsaw–Zürich route. LOT would use a total of 14 ERJ145s, making a total of 300,000 flying hours with 55,000 take-offs and landings.[5]

On 18 November 1999, Minister of the Treasury Emil Wąsacz signed agreements for the sale of 25 per cent of the PLL LOT shares to the Swiss holding company SairGroup, which was already the owner of Swissair. This decision marked the beginning of the privatisation of the Polish airline. Despite the choice of a foreign investor, LOT fully retained its identity and Polish character. Although, that was only the tip of the iceberg. At the time of the agreement, Swissair was already virtually bankrupt. In the 1990s, Swissair had initiated the disastrous 'Hunter Strategy', a major expansion programme devised by the consulting firm of McKinsey & Company. Using this strategy, Swissair aimed to grow its market share through the acquisition of small airlines, rather than entering into alliance agreements. Swissair decided to acquire 49.5 per cent of the successful Italian charter airline Air Europe, the unprofitable Belgian carrier Sabena, as well as significant stakes in Air Liberté, AOM, Air Littoral, Volare, Turkish Airlines, South African Airways, Portugalia and LTU, and a 25 per cent participation in LOT Polish Airlines. It was clear to everyone that Swissair's appetite was much bigger than its mouth could swallow, or its stomach could digest. In the summer of 2000, when Swiss press published a study on the financial situation of the group, the board, for the first time, began to consider scenarios for phasing out the investments and existing participations in other airlines.[6] Emil Wąsacz, who had signed the agreement with Swissair, had already been famous previously for many unsuccessful privatisations, including those of Centrum Department Stores, Telekomunikacja Polska (the Polish telecom giant), and Powszechny Zakład Ubezpieczeń (a large Polish insurance company). Finally, in 2006, Emil Wąsacz appeared before a State Tribunal for corruption, but the court ordered that the evidence be supplemented, delaying a verdict. Despite this, in 2006–07, the Polish government managed to buy back the shares of LOT.

ATR 72s replaced the outdated An-24s. This aircraft was later leased to Eurolot. (Jozef Mols)

Above left: An ATR 72 seen at Frankfurt Airport in 1997. (Aero Icarus Zurich/ CC BY-SA 2.0 Wikimedia Commons Licence)

Above right: LOT ATR 72s were leased to Eurolot. (Piotrus/CC BY-SA 3.0 via Wikimedia Commons Licence)

Left: Later on, Eurolot also obtained the ATR 42-500. (Aero Icarus Zurich/ CC BY-SA 2.0 Wikimedia Commons Licence)

Below: For its regional services, LOT obtained Boeing 737-500s. This one is a 737-55D version. (Jozef Mols)

This Boeing 737-400 serves as publicity for the Polish delegation during the London Olympic Games in 2012. (John Taggart/CC BY-SA 2.0 via Wikimedia Commons Licence)

A LOT Boeing 737-400 on approach. (Kuba Bożanowski/CC BY 2.0 via Wikimedia Commons Licence)

LOT bought a series of Embraer ERJ-145 jets for its regional routes. (ETH Bibliothek Zürich)

Chapter 8

Competition

When the Polish government sold LOT shares to the SairGroup, LOT automatically became a member of the then-nascent Qualiflyer Group. However, this membership would not last long. In 2003, after the collapse of the Qualiflyer Group, the Polish airline joined the Star Alliance. In the meantime, the process of creating an airport as a transit hub – rather than just a destination hub – had started. So, the idea of making Warsaw Chopin Airport (formerly Warsaw-Okęcie Airport) a so-called 'hub' for Central and Eastern Europe made sense. New routes to Zagreb, Tallinn, Bucharest and London Gatwick were started. In order to be able to handle the expected growth in traffic, LOT received 11 aircraft in one year. Indeed in 2000, eight Embraer ERJ145s and three Boeing 737-500s joined the fleet. A year later, LOT transported more than three million passengers. More new connections were launched, including Odessa, Gothenburg, Beirut, as well as a domestic route to Zielona Góra. A year later, flights between Warsaw and Kaliningrad and Bratislava were inaugurated, followed by Poznań–Frankfurt flights. Considering increased operations between Poland and Germany, LOT and Lufthansa signed a preliminary agreement on strategic cooperation and a codeshare agreement for flights between both countries. This agreement opened the way for the Polish carrier to become a member of the Star Alliance. Upon the accession of LOT to the alliance, a Boeing 737-500 (SP-LKE) and a 767 (SP-LPE) received a new promotional livery. At the same time, new codeshare agreements were signed with United Airlines, BMI, Aeroflot and All Nippon Airways (ANA).

Eurolot was also doing well, and LOT signed an agreement with the Italian–French ATR consortium for the delivery of five ATR 42-500 aircraft, replacing older ATR 42-300s it had in its fleet. Around the same time, the airline also obtained two British BAE J31 Jetstream 18-seater aircraft.

As it became clear LOT's passenger numbers would further increase – to over four million passengers by 2004 – the airline signed an agreement with Embraer during the Paris Airshow regarding the delivery of new Embraer 170 jets in standard (ST) configuration. The first (SP-LDA) was delivered on 8 March 2004 and made its first commercial flight on 20 March on the Warsaw–Vienna route. In the following months, several other aircraft of the same type arrived in Warsaw.

At this time, LOT also had to face competition from low-cost airlines operating in Europe, especially ultra-low-cost airlines like Ryanair and Wizz Air, which were particularly successful in the Central European market. Therefore, LOT decided to counter this competition by setting up its own low-cost and charter subsidiary. Centralwings, based in Warsaw, was established in December 2004 and started operations in February 2005, using LOT 737 aircraft. Besides operating flights to a range of Mediterranean beach and island destinations, cities like Amsterdam, Bologna, Lille, Lisbon, Paris, Beauvais and Rome were also served.[1] However, for the majority of the time, about 60 per cent of the capacity was allocated to routes serving Ireland and the UK, in order to compete with Ryanair. In the end, it became clear that Centralwings was not profitable, and the airline ceased operations by the end of 2009. The company was dissolved and reincorporated into LOT.[2] Upon the bankruptcy of Centralwings, LOT established a new charter-only subsidiary under the name of LOT Charters, which made its first commercial flight on 1 June 2009.

Polish low-cost airlines that were attempting to compete with LOT were also facing problems. Air Polonia was the first privately owned low-cost airline in Poland. It had been established in 2001 and started operations in 2003, quickly gaining popularity. With its fleet of Boeing 737 jets, it offered flights from Warsaw to Wrocław, London Stansted and Gdańsk. Flights from Katowice and from Poznań to London Stansted were also available. Air Polonia not only targeted LOT as competition, but also non-Polish carriers flying to Poland like British Airways and Germanwings. Nevertheless, the airline had to cease operations in December 2004 because of financial difficulties.

Air Polonia was not the only Polish competitor. Immediately after freeing the skies over the European Union (EU) in 1997, the rapid process of transforming large old airlines into new entities and the emergence of completely new smaller carriers could begin. One of them was Air Italy, established in 2005 from the ruins of a sister company. The Italian carrier had its base in Rome and had established a strategic cooperation with Alitalia. The airline mainly concentrated on charter flights, and it started to expand its activities to other countries, including Poland. Activities in Poland took place under the brand name Air Italy Poland. Its Polish fleet consisted of a changing range of Boeing jets. Some of them – like the 767-300ER – allowed for very long intercontinental flights. The maintenance of a mixed fleet, including large aircraft, is very expensive, and it is easy to lose financial liquidity. In the end, this would cause the collapse of Air Italy Poland, which had been developed too quickly. One of the worst decisions the airline had taken was the takeover of a direct flight route from Poland to Chicago, from which LOT withdrew for financial reasons in 2010. It turned out to be the nail in the airline's coffin. The carrier, however, would not completely disappear and would be resurrected under the name Air Poland, offering charter flights within Europe.[3]

In a move to replace smaller aircraft with larger ones, LOT decided to buy the Embraer 175, which had a capacity of 82 people. Gradually, these new aircraft – with a staggered delivery schedule between 2009 and 2012 – would replace the Embraer 145 models, which only had a capacity of 48 passengers. As well as a higher capacity, decisive factors included better technical parameters, and, above all, the fact that a good resale price could be obtained for the relatively young 145s. Between April 2006 and September 2010, LOT would receive 14 Embraer 175 jets.

When, in 2006, a new base of operations became available after the reconstruction of the Warsaw Chopin Airport, LOT was in a position to develop its full transit airline potential, as the new airport was much larger than any previous airport in Poland. In order to do so, a new long-haul aircraft was needed. In 2006, the decision was made to obtain Boeing 787-8 Dreamliners under a lease agreement. The airline subsequently ordered seven of these brand-new airliners, with the possibility of extending the order by another six aircraft in the B787-8/-9 versions. The aircraft would be equipped with 18 fully reclining premium seats, 21 reclining premium economy seats and 213 economy seats. At the same time, LOT had signed a codeshare agreement with ANA and Singapore Airlines, thanks to which customers of these airlines could conveniently travel on routes between Asia and Poland. Additionally, an interline ticketing agreement was concluded with British Airways.

In 2008, LOT made the bold decision to open a new route to Beijing in the period before the Olympic Games. In July 2008, the airline signed an agreement with the Polish Olympic Committee that meant LOT had acquired the title of 'Official Carrier of the Polish Olympic Team' for the Beijing games. However, this service would not last for long. As LOT had not received authorisations from Russia for flights over Siberia, the flight to Beijing had to be routed via an air corridor to the south of Kazakhstan. Therefore, the route was too long and, hence, too expensive.

Other new destinations were more successful. Yerevan (Armenia), Beirut, Tallinn, Kaliningrad, Gothenburg and Bratislava had been added to the flight schedule, using the newly acquired Embraer aircraft. Later, flights to Asia were resumed with three weekly flights on the Warsaw–Hanoi route.

On 8 November 2009, LOT launched the first direct transatlantic cargo route in the history of Polish aviation. This initiative became possible thanks to the cooperation between LOT and the Canadian Cargojet airline. A 767-200ER freighter with a capacity of 45 tons of goods was used on the Katowice–Hamilton (Canada)–Katowice route once a week. In 2010, however, LOT cancelled all passenger flights between Kraków and Chicago and New York because of lack of demand and high costs.

Left: In 2004, LOT ordered the Embraer 170. (Jozef Mols)

Below: When LOT joined the Star Alliance, some aircraft like this Embraer were painted in the colours of the alliance. (Embraer)

Other aircraft in the LOT fleet also received the Star Alliance paint scheme. (Aero Icarus Zurich/CC BY-SA 2.0 Wikimedia Commons Licence)

Centralwings was set up as a subsidiary of LOT in order to deal with competition from low-cost carriers. It used LOT's Boeing fleet, like this Boeing 737-300. (Edward Cwik/CC BY-SA 3.0 via Wikimedia Commons Licence)

Above: After a while, Centralwings got its own colour scheme. (Łukasz Golowanow, Maciej Hypś, Konflikty. pl/Wikimedia Commons Licence)

Right: This Centralwings Boeing 737-400 – owned by LOT – clearly shows the Centralwings colours. (Piotrus/ CC BY-SA 3.0 via Wikimedia Commons Licence)

Above: LOT had to face competition from Polish carrier Air Polonia. (Jozef Mols)

Left: Air Italy Polska also became a competitor, using a mixed fleet that included Boeing 737s. (Ken Fielding/https://www.flickr.com/photos/kenfielding, CC BY-SA 3.0 via Wikimedia Commons Licence)

Below: The fleet of competitor Air Italy Polska also included this Boeing 757-200. (Carlos Delgado/CC BY-SA 3.0 via Wikimedia Commons Licence)

Above: When Centralwings ceased operating, the company was reintegrated into LOT, later becoming LOT Charters. (Ken Fielding/https://www.flickr.com/photos/kenfielding, CC BY-SA 3.0 via Wikimedia Commons Licence)

Right: LOT celebrated the 80th anniversary of its foundation in 2009. The event was marked with the application of a gold livery to one of the airline's Boeing 737s. (Eric Salard/CC BY-SA 2.0 via Wikimedia Commons Licence)

Below: This 737-400 received the gold livery following LOT's 80th anniversary. (John Taggart/CC BY-SA 2.0 via Wikimedia Commons Licence)

Chapter 9

Privatisation, Restructuring or Bankruptcy

As LOT had published financial losses over the previous years, the airline decided to separate the Technical Base (maintenance department) from the main structures of the airline. That way the technical service department became a separate company under the name LOT Aircraft Maintenance Services.

However, less-than-brilliant financial results did not prevent the airline from further modernising its fleet. On 11 April 2011, the first of four of the 2008-ordered Embraer 195 medium-range aircraft arrived in Poland – the order was changed from four E175s to E195s. At that time, LOT still had ten E170s and 14 E175s in operation, and five 145s were still in operation, although they had already been put up for sale. In the meantime, two Embraer 175 aircraft had been transferred to the government as VIP aircraft after the Smolensk crash. On 10 April 2010, a Tupolev Tu-154 aircraft operating Polish Air Force Flight 101 crashed near the Russian city of Smolensk, killing all 96 people on board. Among the victims were the president of Poland, Lech Kaczyński, and his wife, the former president of Poland, Ryszard Kaczorowski, the chief of the Polish general staff and other senior Polish military officers, the president of the National Bank of Poland and 18 members of the Polish parliament. The group was arriving from Warsaw to attend an event commemorating the 70th anniversary of the Katyn massacre, a mass murder of Polish intellectuals, politicians and military officers by the Soviets during World War Two. Various conspiracy theories about the crash have since been circulated, but the Russian and Polish officials investigating the crash did not find any evidence supporting this claim. On the other hand, the Polish authorities found serious deficiencies in the organisation and training of the air force unit involved in the crash, which resulted in the transfer of two LOT aircraft to the government in order to provide safe transportation for VIPs.[1]

When the first Embraer 195 arrived, it made its first flight on the LOT network in Europe with a flight to Brussels on 15 April 2011. A second similar aircraft was delivered on 24 June of the same year, with a third one following on 28 August. By the time the aircraft arrived, LOT had applied a new livery pattern, designed by Jacek Bonczek. The navy blue belt line, which was used earlier, had disappeared from the hull, but the inscriptions remained unchanged. The biggest change took place on the vertical tail; the crane bird was now painted in white on a navy blue background with the national colours on the base of the tail. In the same year, LOT had once again received the award in the 'Best Airline in Eastern Europe' category of the *Global Traveler* magazine.

The new CEO of LOT, Marcin Pirog, announced on 5 February 2011 that his airline was considering opening routes to Baku, Sochi, Stuttgart, Oslo, Göthenburg, Dubai, Kuwait and Ostrava from its Warsaw hub in the near future. Previously planned flights to Donetsk in Ukraine had already been inaugurated. The resumption of Beijing flights became feasible following the finalising of an agreement on Siberian overflight permits for LOT by the Polish and Russian governments in November 2011. As a result of the new agreement, LOT received new take-off and landing slots at Moscow's Sheremetyevo International Airport. The same agreement also gave Russian Aeroflot the right to start up flights between Moscow and Kraków. Due to Boeing's limited production capacity, the 787s that had been ordered in 2008 were yet to be delivered and flying to Beijing forced LOT to reconsider its entire long-haul network. The most likely cuts in the timetable would be on flights to Hanoi or one of the airports in the New York area (John F. Kennedy or Newark). The flights to Vietnam were considered to be low-income seasonal activities, whereas Newark Airport is a major Star Alliance hub, and there were prestigious reasons for maintaining flights to John F. Kennedy.[2]

The reader might think that – given the rapid modernisation of the LOT fleet and the positive signals sent out by the airline – LOT was a financially strong company: but this was far from reality. In 2008, the airline had made a loss of PLN 232m (£42.5m), and a year later the loss had increased to PLN 335m (£61.2m). In 2010, the financial losses were 'only' PLN 163m (£29.7m) and PLN 232m (£42.5m) in 2011. Marcin Pirog had to admit that LOT had not been generating profit through the sale of tickets – which is its core business – since the early 1990s. How, then, had the company survived for so long? Primarily, it had been sustained thanks to financial injections provided by the government. One of these injections consisted of the transfer of large blocks of shares in companies from the State Treasury to LOT, such as 1.4 million shares in Bank Pekao, which the carrier sold in 2009. Furthermore, the airline had sold off redundant assets, such as the Centrum LIM high-rise building. Later on, the airline also started selling some of its own divisions. In 2011, LOT Services and LOT Catering were sold. In 2012, LOT sold its stake in LOT Aircraft Maintenance Services to the state-run Agencja Rozwoju Przemysłu (Industrial Development Agency) and also its participation in Petrolot, the energy and oil company. It also decided to sell and lease back the office building where it had its headquarters.[3]

Notwithstanding the fact LOT used all the financial engineering techniques that were available, the airline still had to apply for state aid by 2012. Indeed, this decision was due mainly to the fact that the airline had been left with very limited assets that were not of vital importance to the airline's operations as a carrier. The remaining assets that could be sold, like the 33.3 per cent stake in Casinos Poland, would be difficult to sell. Similarly, the 10-hectare parcel of land near the Warsaw Chopin Airport would be difficult to sell at a price that would be acceptable to the owner, given the poor condition of the European aviation sector at that time.[4]

When LOT applied for state aid, it was not the only European airline that had encountered financial difficulties following the terrorist attacks in New York in 2001, and the massive growth of low-cost airlines in Europe. Europe had already seen bankruptcies of airlines far bigger than LOT. In 2001, Sabena was the first carrier to disappear, followed by Swissair and Air Liberté in France. German Aero Lloyd would follow in 2003. Between 2000 and 2008, no fewer than 79 European airlines had gone bankrupt, of which 14 were in 2004.[5]

Of course, LOT's negative financial results were caused by many different factors. The overly ambitious decision regarding the rapid replacement of the old fleet by mainly leased aircraft had drained cash from the airline, aviation fuel prices had remained high, and Poland was seeing a rapid expansion of low-cost airlines. Paradoxically, the company's ongoing restructuring programme, which had started in 2010 and was supposed to be completed by 2013, had largely contributed to LOT's problems. The company's management board had designed the programme and embarked upon its implementation in response to the company's record loss on its core business in 2009, which was mainly triggered by the soaring oil prices and the weakening of the złoty versus the US dollar (all fuel purchases and aircraft lease payments had to be made in dollars). Fuel invoices constituted about 30 per cent of the carrier's total costs, whereas lease payments constituted nearly 10 per cent. A 10 per cent drop in the value of the złoty versus the dollar would increase the carrier's costs by

PLN 100m (£18.2m).[6] Furthermore, owing to the economic crisis in the rest of the world, demand for business class tickets had decreased.

The original plan, introduced by the management of LOT, had seemed consistent and logical. As the airline had become a major international carrier via its hub at Warsaw Chopin Airport, more passengers could be attracted. The fleet renewal contributed to improved punctuality and regularity of flights. In the first half of 2012, LOT was rated as the most punctual European airline according to data published by the Association of European Airlines. In 2011, the number of LOT's passengers was 9 per cent higher when compared to the previous year. In the first half of 2012, the number of passengers even increased by 13 per cent (the best result among all European airlines, which jointly recorded a 3.9 per cent total average increase in the number of passengers). LOT's occupancy rate had exceeded the European average of 75 per cent. However, all the above mentioned achievements had required substantial expenditure, and LOT had overestimated its own possibilities and exceeded its financial capabilities in a period that was characterised by a worldwide economic downturn.[7]

Fortunately, the European Commission, which oversees state aid in European countries, decided that the sale of LOT's subsidiaries, LOT Services, LOT Catering and LOT Airport Maintenance Services was carried out on market terms and therefore did not involve state aid, as regulated by the EU. As no open and transparent tender had been organised regarding the sale of these subsidiaries, the Commission had to make sure that the sales did not contain hidden subsidies in favour of LOT.[8]

While, on the one hand, LOT was trying to solve its financial problems, the airline also announced its new 'East meets West' strategy in an attempt to improve its financial position ahead of the possible privatisation that was expected in the first half of 2012. The plan would see the carrier increase its focus on connections, using its Warsaw hub to bridge the East and West and, at the same time, attract more passengers for its premium economy offering.[9]

LOT obtained four Embraer 195s in 2011. (LOT Polish Airlines)

Above: A LOT Embraer 195 arriving in Warsaw. (LOT Polish Airlines)

Left: Cabin of the new Embraer 195 jet. (LOT Polish Airlines)

Chapter 10
East meets West

In order to implement the 'East Meets West' plan, LOT needed more modern long-haul aircraft. The airline had ordered the brand-new Boeing 787, which was to be used on routes to China and/or Japan, in 2006 for delivery in 2008, but the deliveries had been delayed multiple times. The airline therefore had started talks already with its Star Alliance partner ANA about helping LOT secure good slots at Tokyo Narita. ANA itself had been the launch customer for the 787, but it did not plan on starting up flights to Warsaw. Therefore, LOT saw an opportunity to launch the route itself under a codeshare agreement with ANA. It was also LOT's intention to use the new 787s on routes to Beijing and possibly even on a route to Hanoi, which had been launched earlier in 2011 with 767 equipment.[1] The selection of Hanoi came as a surprise to many observers, because most foreign carriers flew to larger Ho Chi Minh City, but that was exactly the reason why LOT wanted to become the only European carrier to offer flights to the fast-growing northern Vietnamese market.

In addition to Hanoi, LOT used its fleet of five 767 jets to operate to four North American destinations: Chicago, New York JFK, Newark and Toronto. The airline even chartered a sixth 767 from Air Italy to boost capacity on these routes during the summer peak season. According to an article in the *Chicago Tribune*, LOT announced it would also use the 787 on flights between Warsaw and Chicago once the aircraft had been delivered.[2] Nevertheless, LOT was seeking growth mainly in Asia, and new destinations – including these in America – would be considered later after delivery of the Dreamliners.[3]

Besides flights to Tokyo, Beijing and Hanoi, LOT also opened a route to Donetsk in Ukraine, in order to prove its intention of spreading its network eastwards. The shift in strategy to focus more on transit traffic since the opening of the new airport in Warsaw had already driven an increase in revenues and total traffic. LOT expected to carry more than five million passengers in 2011, up from four-and-a-half million in 2010. The airline hoped to reduce losses for the year 2011 and a return to profitability in 2012.

Notwithstanding good prospects and hope, LOT still had to fight to survive, and the delivery of the 787 was only one cornerstone in the implementation of the 'East Meets West' strategy that was supposed to guarantee a return to profitability. Therefore, the Polish government was looking for partners that would be willing to aid the troubled carrier. At one time, rumours spread that Air China might be interested in partnering with LOT. Poland had indeed been enthusiastically chatting up China, inviting investment as it sought to make itself the Asian giant's premier partner in the EU. However, sources close to Air China made it clear that China would not be interested in obtaining a non-controlling stake in the Polish airline. The problem was that the provisions of the EU laws prevent the acquisition of a majority stake in an airline by an investor from outside the EU.

A few months later, newspapers mentioned that Star Alliance partner Turkish Airlines might be interested in obtaining a participation in LOT. However, some analysts said they saw little logic in a deal to take control of a loss-making Polish flag carrier.[4,5] Both airlines share Western Europe as their key focus market, but they are otherwise completely different carriers. Turkish Airlines has an extensive long-haul network, while LOT's focus was more regional – although LOT's 'East meets West' plan appeared to mesh with Turkish Airlines' strategy.[6] However, the main difference between the airlines was that one was clearly showing a trajectory of growth, while LOT had only been looking to reduce losses and survive. Furthermore, LOT was not the only possible investment target for Turkish Airlines. Turkish had also been considering government-owned CSA Czech Airlines, which had undergone a restructuring process, and also Slovenia's Adria Airways as possible targets.

A few months later, Turkish Airlines dropped its bid for LOT. Unnamed 'unofficial' sources hinted to the sale being dropped because of the EU law, which, as mentioned, outlaws companies from outside the union owning more than 50 per cent of any European airline.[7,8,9] The spokeswoman for Poland's treasury ministry, Magdalena Kobos, told journalists that after the official notice from Turkish Airlines, the government would return to talks with other partners who had declared their interest. However, everybody could predict that LOT did not stand a chance of going through a rapid privatisation process, because, given the condition of the airline industry in Europe at that time, nobody would be willing to take on the huge costs of the company's restructuring process.[10]

While LOT was supposed to be ending 2012 in the black with a probable profit of some £14m, instead the carrier had to rush to the treasury again for a handout just to keep its aircraft flying through Christmas. The airline asked for PLN 1bn (£182m) in aid, whereas the airline only got total revenues of some PLN 3bn (£525m). Obviously, the treasury minister blamed CEO Marcin Pirog for the debacle. The CEO, who had served just over two years – much longer than the average for LOT chief executives during the difficult periods of financial trouble – was removed from the board. Though, without the state aid, LOT would not be able to pay its bills for fuel, airport fees and salaries. A simple change at the top of the airline was not going to save it. The carrier had to face much deeper structural problems, something with which many other small flag carriers were also struggling. In Hungary, national flag carrier Malev had stopped flying in the summer of 2012, while Czech CSA could only survive thanks to a restructuring programme and help from Korean Air and Kuwait Airways. LOT still tried to be a full-service airline, offering long-haul flights to destinations such as Toronto, Chicago and Beijing while flying shorter national and European routes. 'Not every airline can do everything without subsidies', said Aleksander Domarodzki, managing partner of DGL Polska consultancy.[11]

Notwithstanding the financial worries, LOT's first Boeing 787-8 arrived on 16 November 2012, followed by a second one on 21 December. But there were new clouds on the horizon. In January 2013, all Boeing 787s were grounded worldwide by the FAA due to battery failures, causing onboard fires on two aircraft operated by ANA. Nevertheless, LOT would receive its third 787 – this time with new batteries – on 17 May 2013. A fourth 787 arrived on 22 June, and the fifth one on 30 July. It would take until 1 June 2013 for LOT's 787s to take to the air, however. As LOT had sold tickets on transatlantic flights to be operated by the 787 before this time, it had to lease a Boeing 777 from Euro Atlantic Airways from 4 May 2013 to 7 June 2013, together with a cockpit crew. Later, an Airbus A330-200 was leased from Portuguese airline Hi Fly from mid-April to the end of May 2013. As LOT had hoped to introduce the fuel-efficient 787 much earlier, this was another setback for the troubled airline.[12]

The new CEO of LOT, Sebastian Mikosz, was a man in a hurry, racing to turn around the loss-making flag carrier as quickly as possible. He was convinced only privatisation could save the airline. He was the favoured candidate of Treasury Minister Mikołaj Budzanowski, whose job was in danger from enraged Prime Minister Donald Tusk if LOT was not rescued. In order to be able to grant more financial aid to the carrier, the Polish government needed the authorisation from the European Commission, which in turn required a complete restructuring of the airline. At the same time, Mikosz was juggling with a flight schedule thrown into disarray by Boeing's problems with the new 787. The aircraft should have given LOT an advantage on Asian and North American long-haul routes against traditional competitors like Lufthansa and British Airways, as well as the newer Middle East airlines that were starting to carry passengers from Warsaw to Asia through their hubs in the Gulf area. However, Mikosz now had to rely on older 767s, which were more expensive to operate and had fewer lucrative premium and business class seats. The government also had to do its part, changing a law that designated LOT as a strategic company that had to remain under government control. In previous years, the law had scared off potential investors. Of course, layoffs would also be part of the restructuring programme and had to be discussed with the trade unions.[13]

In March 2014, LOT had to eliminate foreign flights from all domestic airports except Warsaw. This was the result of the decision by the European Commission, which made the consent for state aid to LOT conditional on such a decision. Flights from Gdańsk, Katowice, Kraków, Poznań and Wrocław to Düsseldorf, Frankfurt and Munich were abolished, and, in the case of Kraków, also to Rome, Tel Aviv and Vienna. The cancellation of these flights was good news for the rivals of LOT, led by Lufthansa. The opening of the new Brandenburg airport in Berlin was indeed an attractive alternative to Warsaw, especially for passengers from western Poland.

On 29 July 2014, the European Commission stated it approved the restructuring aid for LOT.[14] The state aid amounted to PLN 804m (£146m). According to the Commission, LOT had prepared a credible restructuring plan that should make it a viable company in the near future, without unduly distorting competition in the EU single market.

While LOT was struggling to survive, former subsidiary Eurolot ordered eight new Bombardier Q400 Dash 8 NextGen turboprop aircraft. Another four of these aircraft would join the fleet later. In July 2012, as part of the restructuring plan of LOT, the carrier sold its shares in Eurolot to the Ministry of State Treasury (62.1 per cent) and to Towarzystwo Finansowe Silesia (37.9 per cent).

Right: Finally, the Boeing 787 Dreamliner arrived after long delays. (P. Lorenc/LOT Polish Airlines)

Below: The Boeing 787 was intended to become the backbone of the long-haul fleet, supporting the 'East meets West' strategy. (LOT Polish Airlines)

A LOT Boeing 787 arriving at Heathrow Airport. (Adrian Pingstone/Public Domain via Wikimedia Commons Licence)

A Premium Class cabin on board the 787 Dreamliner. (LOT Polish Airlines)

Eurolot ordered a series of Bombardier Q400 NextGen aircraft for its domestic and regional services. (Eurolot)

Cabin of the Bombardier Q400 NextGen. (Michal Petrykowski/Eurolot)

Chapter 11
Back to Profitability?

In 2014, LOT received the first part of the state aid, made possible by the European Commission. It seemed almost like a birthday present that prevented LOT from going bankrupt. Indeed, in 2014, LOT celebrated its 85th birthday. On that occasion, the airline painted one of its Embraer 175 jets with the characteristic colours of its aircraft from the 1940s. The LOT paint shop soon had more work to do, as, on 23 September, an aircraft was painted in colours inspired by the *Mamma Mia* musical. The airline had become the official carrier of artists for the Polish version of the musical from Teatr Muzyczny Roma. In the meantime, the airline had also received its sixth 787. On 3 September 2014, the airline achieved a record when one of the Dreamliners made the longest direct flight to Antofagasta in Chili, covering over 7,456 miles (12,000km) and spending 14½ hours in the air without interruption. Furthermore, by the end of November, LOT Dreamliners had carried over half a million passengers!

The year 2014 was a positive year for LOT for more than one reason; namely, the airline ended it in the black. With more than PLN 99m (£18.1m) profit on its core business of flying, LOT earned 40 per cent more than it had planned. It was the company's first profit in seven years. The airline was supposed to end 2014 with PLN 70m (£12.8m) profits on its core business but was almost PLN 30m (£5.5m) above the restructuring plan assumptions. Because of the public aid received, LOT had to cut the number of flights by almost 8 per cent in 2014, compared to previous years, as international flights from airports other than Warsaw were cancelled. Nevertheless, the airline carried 2 per cent more passengers and increased revenue while keeping the same cost level. By rebuilding its network of flights, LOT had increased its connecting capacities by over 40 per cent in its Warsaw hub. This was also the first year the airline saw the 'Dreamliner effect', which was not only popular among passengers, but also provided tangible benefits such as fuel savings. Sebastian Mikosz, however, remained cautious. He warned LOT had to remember that this was just one first step of transformation and that more challenges were ahead. The total net profit of the airline, without accounting effects, also remained positive and amounted to PLN 36m (£6.6m). If one takes into account the further effects of the currency exchanges (mainly of the dollar), a minus still appeared in the bookkeeping for a total amount of PLN 263m (£48.1 m). This last figure was only an artificial accounting record, having no effect on the actual financial situation of the company, as LOT's relationship between earnings and spendings in foreign currencies was fairly in balance. Therefore, no currency was in fact exchanged, but the amounts are only booked in PLN according to valid Polish accounting standards.[1]

In a press briefing in Chicago in May 2014, CEO Sebastian Mikosz had pointed out the steps the beleaguered carrier had taken and still had to take in order to return to profitability. The restructuring of the airline had been centred on a mixture of cost discipline and revenue-strengthening initiatives. Cost reduction had been achieved by changing the employee compensation structure from salaries to an hourly pay system and eliminating several positions altogether. LOT had also focused on improving fleet utilisation through increased charter flying. Mikosz noted that LOT had increased the utilisation of its Boeing 787s to nearly 19½ hours per day with charter flying supplementing an already aggressive long-haul programme. Charter services were ideal, as LOT had been banned from launching new scheduled long-haul routes due to the conditions imposed by the European Commission. Therefore, the 787s were used on charter operations to Sri Lanka, Vietnam, Mexico and Cuba. At the same time, the airline was also moving towards a more complex fare structure to boost revenue by more effectively matching price and seat inventory. LOT had also seen a substantial increase in its cargo revenues, thanks in part to the expanded cargo capacity of the 787. The belly capacity of the 787 with twice daily flights to Chicago offered LOT the equivalent cargo capacity of one daily dedicated freighter service.[2]

In 2014, LOT also reached a deal with Boeing regarding compensation for its 787 Dreamliner problems. The deal was reached after long negotiations that did not appear to be headed in a direction the airline was happy with. As a result, LOT threatened to take Boeing to court. In order to avoid an embarrassing appearance in court over the aircraft type and its many shortfalls, Boeing decided to agree upon a compensation package that comprised a mix of cash compensation plus the guarantee of future lower lease rates.[3]

As discussed, the authorisation by the European Commission regarding state aid to LOT Polish Airlines also stipulated restrictions on fleet and route growth. However, considering the positive evolution of its financial situation, LOT estimated it would not need the total amount of the aid for which it first had asked. The airline hoped to be able to expand its fleet by the end of 2015. At the end of 2014, LOT was operating a fleet of 37 aircraft, including three Boeing 737-400s (primarily used on charters), ten Embraer E170s, 12 E175s, six E195s and six 787-8 Dreamliners. Eurolot, on the other hand, operated a fleet of 11 Bombardier Q400 turboprops with three additional airframes on order. Over the previous decade, LOT had operated a large fleet of older aircraft. As its finances deteriorated, five 737-400s, six 737-500s, five E145s and six 767-300Ers had been retired. Eurolot had operated eight ATR 72-200s and five ATR 42-500s. When 16 aircraft were retired, they had been replaced by only six new jets. This reduction in the fleet led to a network pull back, with LOT withdrawing many point-to-point services from secondary Polish cities, such as Kraków, and centralising in a core hub in Warsaw. Once the European Commission gave the green light, LOT intended to add new aircraft to its fleet. Sebastian Mikosz hinted strongly at a new order for either the Boeing 737 MAX or the Airbus A320neo.[4] It will come as no surprise that Mikosz also stated – during the Airlines in Transition Conference on 25 and 26 March 2015 – that his airline was looking for new investors from within the EU.[5]

As stated earlier, LOT had sold its shares in Eurolot in an attempt to improve its financial position; however, the airline now badly needed a partner to provide connecting flights to its international network. Therefore, LOT and Eurolot signed a codeshare cooperation agreement that would make it much easier for both LOT and Eurolot passengers to travel within the network of connections of both carriers. The agreement concerned the cooperation of both carriers on almost all routes served by Eurolot.[6] The agreement would, however, not last for long. On 6 February 2015, it was announced Eurolot would be liquidated due to financial problems and would end operations on 31 March 2015. LOT Polish Airlines would subsequently assume some of Eurolot's routes, re-leasing former Eurolot aircraft.

Notwithstanding the positive evolution of LOT's financial results, the Supreme Audit Office of Poland was not entirely pleased with the results obtained by the airline or by the means with which this performance was obtained. The Office clearly stated that the public aid, granted to LOT, saved the company from bankruptcy, and the implemented restructuring plan resulted in only a partial improvement in the financial situation. Therefore, in the opinion of the Office, the obtained results did not give grounds to conclude that the existence of the airline was not in danger or that it would achieve sustainable profitability and, as a consequence, generate profits, which was the purpose of granting state aid. According to the Office, well-thought-out and long-term decisions were still needed. The Office was also very critical of the restructuring process of LOT prior to the granting of public aid. Income and costs were unrealistically planned, and subsequent restructuring programmes were created without a thorough analysis of the reasons for the problems encountered. Furthermore, a mess in the storage of documents and contracts and carelessness in spending money on advisory services came to light. The Office concluded that LOT's situation – even after the granting of state aid – remained serious and, without finding an investor, its chances of surviving in the extremely competitive aviation market remained slim.[7]

This Embraer jet received a special historic paint scheme to celebrate LOT's birthday. (Anna Podkaminer-Lewandowska/LOT Polish Airlines)

This Embraer 175 provides publicity for the *Mamma Mia* musical, performed by a Polish musical company. (LOT Polish Airlines)

When Eurolot ceased operations, LOT re-leased the former Eurolot Bombardier Q400 Dash turboprops. (LOT Polish Airlines)

This former Eurolot Bombardier Q400 did not receive the standard LOT colours. (LOT Polish Airlines)

Chapter 12

Expansion

Although the report from the Supreme Audit Office was casting doubts about LOT's future, 2016 saw the airline on the road to expansion. The airline reversed three years of capacity declines by growing its annual seat capacity by 23 per cent, with a total of over seven-and-a-half million seats. This was primarily because the airline was allowed to resume services on a number of routes that it had been forced to suspend as part of the conditions imposed by the European Commission. As these restrictions were lifted in early 2016, the airline could launch no fewer than six routes in the first days of the year. Later, another 14 routes were launched or resumed until the end of September. Some ten years earlier, LOT accounted for almost 40 per cent of all seats offered at Polish airports, with its low-cost carrier Centralwings adding another 6 per cent. Under pressure from the rise of low-cost carriers, its share had dropped to some 23 per cent in 2015. However, starting in 2016, this trend was reversed, and LOT managed to once again increase its market share.[1]

In January 2016, LOT had added Barcelona, Zürich, Zagreb, Düsseldorf, Chisinau, Belgrade and Yerevan to its route map. That same month, LOT's first airlink arrived in Tokyo Narita. A few days later, LOT's first aircraft arrived in Venice. March saw the opening of connections to Ljubljana, Luxembourg, Kharkov, Athens, Beirut, Nice, Cluj Napoca, Palanga and Kosice. A month later, in April, the airline resumed its flights to Brussels. In October 2016, LOT inaugurated a direct connection between Warsaw and Seoul in South Korea.

In order to attract more passengers, having a broad network of connections is obviously a necessity, but also good in-flight service is essential. In April, LOT started the modernisation of its Boeing 737-400 jets in order to raise passenger comfort. On 13 October 2016, Air Lease Corporation confirmed the placement of six Boeing 737-MAX 8 aircraft with LOT, together with five more options for aircraft of the same type. Deliveries would start in 2017.

Expansion of its own network of destinations was not the only way in which LOT tried to grow. When Estonian Airlines went bankrupt, the Estonian government decided to set up a new airline under the name of Nordic Aviation Group AS, with its base at Tallinn Airport. On 30 March 2016, the name was changed to Nordica. In the first year, Slovenian Adria Airways operated most of Nordica's flights while Nordica built up its fleet and crews. The agreement was, however, valid for only one year and was not renewed. In November 2016, LOT and Nordica announced a strategic cooperation, including a 49 per cent participation by the Polish airline in Nordica's subsidiary Regional Jet. This subsidiary was responsible for the day-to-day operations of Nordica.[2] As a result of the cooperation, LOT obtained the right to put its flight number on Nordica flights departing from Stockholm to Tallinn and Warsaw. This made it possible for LOT to offer connecting flights between Sweden and Estonia on the one hand and destinations on LOT's route map on the other hand.[3] Besides this cooperation, LOT also extended its codeshare agreement with Japanese carrier ANA in such a way that LOT passengers to Tokyo would be able to connect with ANA's flights from Tokyo to Sapporo, Sendai and Fukuoka. By the end of 2016, LOT proudly announced it had transported more than five million passengers that year.

In the next year, 2017, LOT further expanded its activities. Flights from Kraków to Chicago were resumed, followed by a direct connection from Warsaw to Los Angeles in April and one from Warsaw to Newark a few days later. On 30 May, the Polish carrier also started its route to Astana in Kazakhstan on the occasion of the Astana Expo 2017, where LOT and subsidiary LOT Travel were official partners. In June, LOT opened five connections to Tel Aviv from Lublin, Gdańsk, Poznań, Wrocław and Warsaw. In the meantime, the first new Boeing 737-800 NG had joined the fleet, together with the seventh 787-800. On 15 July, the eighth Dreamliner arrived. The arrival of these big passenger aircraft made it possible to not only offer scheduled flights, but the aircraft were also used on charter flights to long-haul destinations like Rio de Janeiro and Panama.

By the end of 2017, it became clear LOT was slowly recovering, although its position remained fragile. That year, the airline had increased its sales revenue by some 32 per cent compared to 2016. These dynamics were consistent with the increase in seat offering, which amounted to 31.8 per cent. On long-haul flights, the increase in offering amounted to 36 per cent. Of course, the airline also had to pay higher costs, and these had gone up by 31 per cent compared to 2016. In the end, it became clear LOT had made a profit of PLN 273m (£49.5m). By the end of the year, the airline employed 331 pilots, 569 flight attendants and 702 ground workers.[4] The managers of LOT started evaluating the economics of future narrow-body and wide-body acquisitions to broaden expansion initiatives. Several aircraft types, including the Airbus A220, Embraer E-Jet-E2 families, the Dreamliner and the Airbus A350 XWB were studied.[5] In April 2018, the airline announced it had ordered three additional Boeing 787-9 aircraft, bringing the total of the -9 variant to seven of the 15 787s expected to be in the fleet by October 2019.

The year 2018 saw a further expansion of the network. On 9 March, a direct flight from Rzeszów to Tel Aviv was inaugurated. This was the sixth route from Poland to Israel operated by LOT. Later in the year, El Al and LOT would sign a codeshare agreement on flights between the two countries. Also in March, LOT launched direct flights between Warsaw and Oslo, followed by a direct flight between Kraków and Budapest. On 30 April, LOT opened its tenth connection to the United States by starting a direct Rzeszów–Newark route. In May, flights to Singapore were initiated. On 1 June, connections to Podgorica and Skopje were opened. Also in May, LOT started up scheduled flights from outside Poland, beginning with long-haul flights to New York and Chicago from Budapest in Hungary. A year later, the airline would start flying from Vilnius to London City Airport and from Tallinn to Brussels and Stockholm. In June, Domodedovo Airport was added to LOT's route network. It was the second airport in the capital of Russia on a Polish airline schedule. To be able to further expand, LOT ordered an additional six Boeing 737 MAX 8s. This way, the airline would operate a total of 12 of these aircraft. When Poland celebrated the centenary of Poland regaining its independence in June, one of the Boeing 737 MAX 8 aircraft, as well as a Dreamliner, were presented with a white and red paint scheme as a reference to the Polish flag. In July, LOT signed a codeshare agreement with Air China, thanks to which the number of direct connections between Warsaw and Beijing increased from three to eight flights a week.

As the airline was slowly recovering from financial problems of the past, but at the same time had to finance its expansion, it was decided in October 2018 that Aircraft Maintenance Services, LS Airport Services and LS Technics would be inducted in the Polish Aviation Group (Polska Grupa Lotnicza), consolidating key aviation companies that were owned by the Polish State Treasury. By the end of the year, LOT announced that it had served eight million passengers for the first time in its history. Revenues of sales amounted to PLN 6.19bn (£1.15bn).

To celebrate the centenary of Poland's independence, this Boeing 787-9 received a special red and white paint scheme. (A. Grochal/LOT Polish Airlines)

Above: The centenary Boeing 787-9 is seen at Warsaw. (Andrzej Otrebski/CC BY-SA 4.0 via Wikimedia Commons Licence)

Left: Painting the tail of the 787-9 in centenary colours. (LOT Polish Airlines)

Above: Also this Boeing 737 MAX 8
received the special centenary paint
scheme. (LOT Polish Airlines)

Right: LOT took a 49 per cent
participation in Nordica. This
Bombardier CRJ-900ER clearly shows
the names of both companies. (Ad
Meskens/CC BY-SA 4.0 via Wikimedia
Commons Licence)

Below: A CRJ-900ER in the Nordica
colors with the LOT title on the
fuselage. (Rosedale 7175/CC BY-SA
2.0 via Wikimedia Commons Licence)

Besides the CRJ-900ERs, Nordica also operated ATR equipment. (Anna Zvereva/CC BY-SA 2.0 via Wikimedia Commons Licence)

The LOT crews have the task of making passengers feel at home on board the flight. (LOT Polish Airlines)

LOT desks at the Warsaw Chopin Airport. (Rakoon/CC0 via Wikimedia Commons Licence)

An aircraft undergoing maintenance. (LOT Polish Airlines)

Chapter 13
Turning Points

By 2019, it had become clear LOT had survived its financial problems – thanks to government aid – and could further expand its operations as European restrictions were lifted. The results became clearly visible in the accounts the airline published by the end of the year. It had carried more than ten million passengers and had launched 15 new destinations. Its sales revenues had increased to PLN 7.37bn (£1.4bn), and profits before taxation had reached PLN 91.9m (£17m). The greatest growth in the number of passengers was on long-haul flights (up 30.4 per cent). In the case of short- and medium-haul flights, there were 11.4 per cent more passengers than the previous year. Domestic routes only saw a growth of 4.7 per cent.[1,2] As part of LOT's expanding network, the airline launched direct flights to Beijing's second airport – Beijing Daxing – on 16 January 2020.

These results were obtained notwithstanding two major problems. First of all, the 737 MAX worldwide grounding hit the entire airline industry, resulting in major disruptions, caused by problems with the new type of aircraft. Also, another Boeing aircraft type was hit by malfunctions. The Rolls Royce engines used in the Dreamliner were not trouble-free. Both aircraft types were used by LOT and could be considered as the backbone of the medium- and long-haul operations. At the time of the grounding, LOT should have had nine 737 MAX aircraft at its disposal, and the grounding resulted in an unexpected financial burden as they had to be replaced by other (leased) aircraft. Nevertheless, Rafał Milczarski (the current CEO of LOT and the Polish Aviation Group) remained optimistic. He hoped his airline would see its number of passengers grow to 25 million by the time the new Central Communication Hub would open in 2027.[3] The Communication Hub is a new, built-from-scratch airport to be located approximately 25 miles (40km) southwest of Warsaw and will replace the Warsaw Chopin Airport, which is slowly starting to be surrounded by urban areas. At first, the airport would have two runways, but ultimately four. The combined airport and train station is planned to initially serve 40 million passengers per year and ultimately around 100 million.[4]

In the meantime, LOT's subsidiary Nordica had announced it would terminate all scheduled operations from its homebase in Tallinn in order to focus on leasing operations for other airlines. Key routes were taken over by LOT. In February 2020, Nordica was rebranded as Xfly, and the airline decided to obtain an additional seven Embraer 190/195s on leasing contracts in order to expand its operations.[5]

LOT was also trying to obtain expansion in other ways. On 24 January 2020, news agency Reuters announced that LOT was acquiring Thomas Cook's German airline Condor, creating a leading aviation group in Europe. According to sources, the German carrier was sold for about €300m (£254m). Condor operated a fleet of more than 50 aircraft, while LOT had a fleet of over 80.[6] Earlier, and, following the collapse of Thomas Cook, Condor had received a lifeline from Germany in the form of a €380m (£321m) bridging loan. Polish sources made it clear that Condor would continue to be run by the current management and would continue to use its well-established brand name. The airline would become part of the Polish Aviation Group, and it was hoped that Condor might even become the central pillar of the tourism activities of the group. According to Rafał Milczarski, it would be necessary to replace Condor's fleet of Boeing 767 aircraft with more modern jets. A further fleet expansion was also not ruled out.[7]

A few months later, however, catastrophe hit the worldwide aviation industry when the COVID-19 pandemic forced airlines to either completely or partially shut down operations. On 16 March 2020, LOT had to suspend its operations. In the light of this new situation, LOT withdrew from buying Condor, which highlights the understandable anxiety among airlines to commit any funds beyond what was needed for immediate survival in lockdown.[8] During the lockdown, Condor asked for an additional €200m (£169m) in state aid and continued operating repatriation flights.[9] A few months later, Condor sued the Polish Aviation Group for the abandoned takeover by LOT.[10] Condor wanted to obtain €55.8m (£47.2m) in damages after the group withdrew from the agreement. LOT, however, maintained that Condor 'breached obligations resulting from the investment agreement' and that the Aviation Group's decision to pull out therefore remained 'both effective and legitimate'. At the same time, however, LOT also indicated that the worsening coronavirus pandemic in Europe was also a factor affecting its decision.

Due to the pandemic, the airline dipped into the red. Poland was one of the first countries in Europe to suspend flights, and even when connections reopened, many Poles opted for domestic holidays, and foreign visitor numbers were down significantly. Domestic flights had restarted on 1 June 2020, whereas international flights were resumed on a very limited basis from 1 July 2020. Over the entire year, the number of passengers declined by 70 per cent to 3.1 million, and the number of charter flights plunged by 73 per cent. The total loss of the airline was higher than the accumulated profits of the previous four years put together.[11, 12]

In October, LOT had to put in a request for PLN 4.5bn (£834m) of public financing to help cover losses during the pandemic. In July 2021, LOT had already recorded a net loss of £269m. By December, the European Commission approved two Polish measures for a total of about €650m (£550m) to support the airline in the context of the coronavirus outbreak. Two thirds of the aid consisted of a subsidised loan to be granted by the Polish Development Fund, and the rest concerned a capital injection by the Polish government.[13] As a result of the capital injection, the State Treasury would have a participation of 69.30 per cent of the LOT shares, whereas the Polish Aviation Group would be holding 30.7 per cent. But one has to realise that the Polish Aviation Group is fully owned by the State Treasury.[14,15]

A LOT Polish Airlines aircraft at the Warsaw Chopin Airport. The airline hopes to move to a brand-new airport in 2027. (LOT Polish Airlines)

A LOT Embraer jet undergoing maintenance. (LOT Polish Airlines)

A LOT Embraer E175 seen at Albrecht Dürer Airport in Nurnberg. (Albrecht Dürer Airport Nurnberg)

Colorful paint schemes increased the visibility of LOT at foreign airports. (LOT Polish Airlines).

Right: LOT's Nordica subsidiary decided to halt all scheduled flights and to concentrate on charter and lease business. (Daniel Czyk/ Wikimedia Commons Licence)

Below left: Thanks to the introduction of the Dreamliner, LOT obtained a large cargo capacity. (LOT Polish Airlines)

Below right: Loading cargo aboard a LOT Boeing 787 Dreamliner. (LOT Polish Airlines)

Chapter 14

Rebuilding the Network

The grounding of the Boeing 737 MAX and 787, as well as the COVID pandemic were difficult to digest for LOT and other airlines around the world. In order to defend itself against the consequences of these problems, LOT made some important decisions.

First of all, LOT decided to sell its 49 per cent share in Xfly, the subsidiary of Nordica. Nordica itself took over the LOT shares in its subsidiary, which operates as a capacity-provider. However, both airlines stressed that commercial cooperation between them would continue.[1] Aside from decreasing LOT's liabilities towards the Baltic carrier, the measure was also imposed by the European Commission as a condition to approve state aid to Nordica in its home country in light of the coronavirus pandemic.

An even more important decision came up regarding the grounding of the 737 MAX fleet between March 2019 and March 2021. At the time of the grounding, the Polish carrier had five 737 MAX aircraft in its fleet. The airline argued that the grounding of its delivered aircraft and the deferral of planned deliveries during the period of LOT's rapid expansion pre-COVID led to substantial losses as it forced the airline to wet lease multiple other aircraft through costly short-term deals. The Boeing 737 MAX aircraft were leased from the US Export-Import Bank. Although LOT had requested compensations for the grounding of its aircraft, Boeing refused such claims. The manufacturer stated that the lease contract with the financial institution did not clearly give any guarantee in case of technical problems. Earlier, Boeing had also refused to pay damages to LOT concerning the grounding of its 787s due to engine problems. As a result of Boeing's refusal, the relationship between Boeing and LOT soured. The airline made it clear it would not take delivery of another two Boeing 787-9 aircraft it had ordered through lessors and put in storage in the US during the COVID-19 pandemic. The airline also started up talks with lessors about the cancellation or renegotiation of the terms of its outstanding Boeing 737-8 commitments.[2] According to some Polish sources, LOT decided not to buy Boeing products in the future. The airline had been a loyal customer of the American manufacturer, but now considered starting negotiations with Airbus regarding future deliveries.[3,4]

LOT's Chief Operating Officer Maciej Wilk stated LOT had focused on lease concessions instead of short-term deferrals or payment waivers during the COVID-19 pandemic. In his opinion, this is better from a long-term perspective, because the airline believes that, once air traffic comes back, there will be a huge overcapacity in the market, and price competition would be more intense than in the past. Therefore, airlines would need to find effective cost reductions. In exchange for lessors' concessions, LOT was offering lease extensions. According to Wilk, operators would have to phase out older generation jets as a result of European green policies. These aircraft would have to be replaced by newer types, which would be more fuel-efficient and therefore cleaner. As LOT is one of the largest Embraer operators, with a current fleet of 37 aircraft and with Q400s as well, Wilk realised all these aircraft would have to be replaced as they are less fuel efficient. To do so, the airline had defined two options – one being the Embraer E2, while the other would be the Airbus A220, which offers flexibility due to the available variants. Replacing older aircraft with new ones will of course also require communication with aftermarket service providers.[5]

From an operational point of view, LOT performed surprisingly well during the pandemic, which lasted much longer than predicted. In 2021, the airline transported 4.2 million passengers. The regularity of operations was 99.7 per cent, and punctuality increased to 86 per cent. Of course, LOT admitted that, due to successive variants of the coronavirus and the uncertainty of travel, the air transport market did not recover as fast as hoped. LOT used this time to expand its activities in the holiday market. Thanks to cooperation with travel agents, the airline has completed four times more charter operations than in 2020. Among the operations that started up again, one can mention flights from Poznań to Palma de Majorca and from Burgas and Wrocław to Barcelona. The accelerating pace of vaccinations in Europe and the gradual loosening of restrictions by European countries enabled the airline to be cautiously optimistic.[6] As far as scheduled operations are concerned, flights to Paris and Vilnius were very popular, while Tirana (Albania) turned out to be the most desirable.[7] Thanks to the lifting of entry restrictions to New York and Chicago, the number of guests on board its transatlantic flights returned to the 2019 level.[8]

When presenting the new flight network for the winter holidays on 18 November 2021, the airline stated it would offer a total of nearly 100 routes. The airline's priority was to reconstruct its flight network in order to return as quickly as possible to flying as it was before the pandemic. Besides the European destinations, LOT announced it would soon reinstate its Warsaw–Miami flights after a long break caused by the pandemic. According to LOT, the opening up of the US market is of key importance for the revival of passenger traffic. Flights to Florida will be operated by Boeing 787s. At the same time, the airline announced it would offer flights to Colombo in Sri Lanka, also to be operated by 787s.[9] Earlier, in April 2021, the airline had already indicated it would add a new destination to its network. From September 2021, the airline would fly to Dubai, using 737-800NGs as well as Dreamliners. LOT would inaugurate this connection just before the opening of the World Expo 2020. Dubai had become one of the Poles' favourite winter exotic destinations. Before the pandemic, in 2019 alone, almost 100,000 Poles had travelled from Poland to Dubai.[10] The Polish entry to the market would come four days before low-cost carrier Flydubai intended to begin service on this route. Furthermore, Emirates already operates six flights from Poland per week using its 777-300ER. Given this number of flights, it is clear the market between Poland and the Persian Gulf is set to become more crowded, increasing competition and downward pressure on ticket prices.[11] To complete the list of announced connections, it is good to mention that LOT is also planning to resume flights from Budapest airport to New York JFK in June 2022. Before the pandemic, these flights had been very popular. Besides carrying passengers, LOT's 787s can also carry up to 12 tonnes of cargo in both directions.[12]

While the carrier was trying to reconstruct its network, geopolitical events also forced it to adapt its route map. Due to tensions in Belarus, the airline had decided to suspend its flights to Minsk in May 2021. This decision also affected its flights to Moscow, which had to be rerouted over Lithuania and Latvia. Flights to Asia – once fully resumed – would have to take place in the same way, or alternatively over Romania, Bulgaria and Turkey.[13]

This small change to LOT's reconstruction path could, however, not dampen the optimism of the carrier. In 2020, rumours suggested that the governments of Poland, the Czech Republic, Hungary and Slovakia were discussing the possibility of creating a single airline to serve Central Europe. These four EU members are also part of the Visegrád Group. Together, their population rivals the UK, France and Italy. Between them, the four countries account for half the seat capacity in Central Europe. In addition, the three biggest airports in Central Europe – Warsaw Chopin, Prague and Budapest – are located within the Visegrád-area. Following the collapse of Malev and the difficulties experienced by CSA Czech Airlines, Central Europe lacks an airline with a truly global scale. LOT is – in comparison to the other Visegrád airlines – the one with the largest international and intercontinental network, and it might, therefore, take the lead in the new airline. But one has to remain cautious. History has tended not to be kind to intergovernmental cross-border airlines.[14]

In the meantime, however, LOT will have to face other challenges. As Europe's airlines look beyond the Omicron variant of the coronavirus to what they hope will be a successful summer season, fuel is the focus as jet fuel prices reach record highs. The IATA has recorded the price for jet fuel as US$105.7 per barrel on 28 January 2022! A young and fuel-efficient fleet will be necessary to overcome this economic challenge.[15]

LOT has its own flight academy for pilot training. (LOT Polish Airlines)

For initial training, LOT uses the Tecnam P 2008 JC. (LOT Polish Airlines)

Above: The Tecnam P 2006T is used for twin-engine training. (LOT Polish Airlines)

Right: LOT 's Boeing 737 MAX fleet was grounded for a long time. (Raymond Zammit)

Below: The Boeing 787 also had to be grounded for some time, because of problems with the engines. (Raymond Zammit)

LOT used several special paint schemes, like the one on this leased Embraer ERJ 195LR. (Raymond Zammit)

The Discover Podkarpackie scheme was introduced on this Embraer 195 in 2021. (S. Fusnik/LOT Polish Airlines)

The Warmia Mazury paint scheme was applied in 2020 on this Embraer ERJ 195. (LOT Polish Airlines)

The Grześki (chocolate brand) paint scheme was applied on this Embraer ERJ 195 in 2019. (Raymond Zammit)

The Śliwka Nałęczowska (an aromatic plum and chocolate flavoured sweet) paint scheme appeared in 2019. (LOT Polish Airlines)

This Embraer 170 had already received a special paint scheme in 2014. (LOT Polish Airlines)

As a result of the dispute with Boeing over the 737 MAX 8 grounding, the commitments for delivery of further 737-800s were renegotiated. (Raymond Zammit)

Incidents and Accidents

(Based upon information from Accident Safety Network)

Crashes

On 1 December 1936, a LOT Lockheed Model 10 Electra (SP-AYB) hit a tree near Malakasa in Greece due to fog. A pilot was killed, and 6 passengers were injured.

On 28 December 1936, a LOT Lockheed Model 10 Electra (SP-AYA) crashed near Suszec in Poland due to icing. Two passengers and a pilot died, and three people were injured.

On 11 November 1937, a LOT Lockheed Model 10 Electra (SP-AYD) crashed near Warsaw during its landing approach in bad weather. Four passengers were killed.

On 23 November 1937, a LOT Douglas DC-2 (SP-ASJ) crashed in Bulgaria's Pirin Mountains while operating a scheduled flight from Thessaloniki to Warsaw via Sofia. The accident happened in bad weather conditions. All six occupants of the aircraft died.

On 22 July 1938, a LOT Lockheed 14H Super Electra (SP-BNG) crashed into a hill at Negrileasa, near Stulpicani in Romania, in bad weather, killing all 14 on board. The cause of the crash was unknown, but the aircraft was most probably struck by lightning. The aircraft was operating a scheduled Warsaw–Lwów–Czerniowce–Bucharest–Thessaloniki passenger flight.

On 18 August 1938, a LOT Lockheed 14H Super Electra (SP-BNJ) was destroyed by fire in Bucharest after one of its tyres burst and the left wing struck the ground. There were no casualties.

On 24 July 1940, a LOT Lockheed 14H Super Electra (SP-BPK) was deliberately crashed in Băneasa, Bucharest. The ex-Imperial Airways (G-AGAA) aircraft had been sold to LOT on 20 March 1939 and seized by Romania on 2 September 1939 at the outbreak of World War Two.

On 26 May 1948, a LOT Lisunov Li-2T (SP-LBC) was damaged beyond repair in a crash landing near Popowice. Nobody was injured.

On 28 March 1950, a LOT Douglas DC-3 (SP-LCC) was damaged beyond repair in a crash landing. There were no injuries.

On 29 March 1950, a LOT Lisunov Li-2 (SP-LBA) was destroyed in a crash. There were no injuries.

On 15 November 1951, a LOT Lisunov Li-2 (SP-LKA) crashed in bad weather and low visibility conditions near Tuszyn, killing all 15 passengers and crew. The aircraft had arrived from Łódź in Poland. Because of engine problems, the pilot elected to discontinue the next flight leg to Kraków. However, the pilot was supposedly forced to continue the flight by officers of the Polish Department of Security.

On 19 May 1952, a LOT Lisunov Li-2 (SP-LBD) was damaged beyond repair in a crash landing near Sowina. There were no injuries.

On 18 July 1952, a LOT Ilyushin Il-12 (SP-LHC) was written off in a crash landing at the Warsaw-Okęcie Airport. There were no injuries

On 15 March 1953, a LOT Douglas DC-3 (SP-LCH) crashed near Katowice. There were no injuries.

On 19 March 1954, a LOT Lisunov-Li2 (SP-LAH) collided with a hill near Gruszowiec following the blackout of the Dąbrowa Tarnowska radio navigation beacon, causing the aircraft to go off course. One passenger died in the crash.

On 14 April 1955, a LOT Lisunov Li-2 (SP-LAE) crashed near Katowice. All 15 passengers survived.

On 14 June 1957, LOT Flight 232 from Warsaw to Moscow, operated by an Ilyushin Il-14 (SP-LNF), crashed during approach to Moscow's Vnukovo International Airport in bad weather and visibility conditions. Five of the eight passengers and four of the five crew members died.

On 11 April 1958, a LOT Convair CV-240 (SP-LPB) crash-landed near Warsaw and was damaged beyond repair after it had lost one propeller mid-flight. There were only four people on board, who had operated a training flight with the aircraft: all of them survived.

On 25 August 1960, a LOT Lisunov Li-2 (SP-LAL) crashed near Tczew while on a survey flight over the Vistula River floods, killing all six people on board.

On 19 December 1962, a LOT Vickers Viscount 804 (SP-LVB) crashed while on approach to Warsaw-Okęcie Airport, having encountered a stall situation, killing all 28 passengers and five crew members on board. The aircraft had been on a scheduled flight from Brussels to Warsaw with an intermediate stop in East Berlin.

On 16 December 1963, a LOT Lisunov Li-2T (SP-LBG) was damaged beyond repair when it undershot the runway on landing at Warsaw-Okęcie Airport after a flight from Rzeszów. The aircraft crashed 100 yards before the runway. The 12 passengers and three crew on board survived.

On 20 August 1965, a LOT Vickers Viscount (SP-LVA) crashed near Jeuk (Belgium) during a thunderstorm while on a ferry flight from Lille (France) to Wrocław. The four people on board perished. The overall atmospheric conditions in the vicinity of the crash site and the circumstances of the accident were such that it was assumed that the pilot lost control of the aircraft when entering a cumulonimbus cloud. It is possible, and even highly probable, that turbulence was a determining factor in the accident.

On 24 January 1969, a LOT Antonov AN-24 (SP-LTE) collided with trees during a landing attempt at Wrocław in poor visibility conditions and crashed. All of the 44 passengers and four crew members on board of Flight 149 from Warsaw to Wrocław survived. The accident was attributed to the decision of the pilot in command to carry out an approach in weather conditions below the minimum limits prescribed for Wrocław Airport, and his non-observance of the prescribed altitude over the outer-radio beacon while performing the approach procedure. The co-pilot did not prevent the pilot from violating flight rules.

On 2 April 1969, a LOT Antonov An-24W (SP-LTF) crashed into Polica, a mountain near Zawoja. The aircraft, with 48 passengers and five crew on board, had been operating Flight 165 from Warsaw to Kraków when the pilots lost orientation because of a snowstorm. There were no survivors.

On 19 April 1973, a LOT Antonov An-24 (SP-LTN) crashed during a training flight near Rzeszów.

On 13 May 1977, a LOT Antonov An-12 (SP-LZA) operating a cargo flight from Warsaw to Beirut via Varna (Bulgaria) crashed near Aramoun (Lebanon), killing all nine people on board, some of whom were agents of the communist Polish secret service. The Antonov departed from Varna, and when approaching Beirut, it was cleared to land on Runway 21 ADF approach and descend to 1,500ft. Language difficulties forced Beirut Area Control to repeat the instructions, but nothing was heard from the flight. There was a lot of controversy about the accident. In September 1966, two Soviet AN-12 military aircraft were delivered to the 13th Transport Aviation Regiment in Kraków. After a year, both aircraft were painted in the colours of LOT and were given civilian markings, but nevertheless only experienced military pilots, dressed in LOT uniforms, sat at the controls. On the day of the crash, two additional passengers boarded the aircraft, together with the crew. The passengers wore plain clothes but were known to the crew as secret agents. Officially, they were employees of Animex (a large meat company), and they were supposed to deliver the 12 tons of veal lying in the hold of the aircraft. The destination was civil war-torn Lebanon, and Beirut was not a safe airport. The guidance systems were not working, and there was no ground control. The Warta insurance company, which paid PLN 28m (£4.9m) in compensation to LOT, discovered the aircraft was not only transporting veal, but also weapons. In the past months, the two civilian-registered AN-12 aircraft had made more than 60 flights to Beirut, with food, medicines, but most of all weapons and ammunition. According to some Polish officers, Poland was trading weapons in Lebanon to obtain dollars with which they were paying for the two Antonov aircraft. No documents related to the disaster near Beirut have been preserved. All traces of SP-LZA also disappeared from the archives of LOT. The official crash report was never released.[1]

On 23 January 1980, a Tupolev Tu-134 (PS-LGB) was damaged beyond repair when it overshot the runway on landing at Warsaw-Okęcie Airport and erupted into flames.

On 14 March 1980, LOT Flight 7 from New York City to Warsaw crashed during a landing attempt at Warsaw-Okęcie Airport, killing all 77 passengers and ten crew members on board the Ilyushin IL-62 (SP-LAA). The pilots had encountered a landing gear problem and began the standard go-around procedure. When power was increased, a shaft in the number 2 engine disintegrated, damaging the rudder and elevator control lines, while causing the aircraft to enter an uncontrolled dive. The aircraft struck the ground in a 20-degree nose down attitude and burst into flames some 2,600ft short of the runway 15 threshold. Metal fatigue in a turbine disc may have caused the accident.

On 26 March 1981, a LOT Antonov An-24 (SP-LTU) crash-landed near Słupsk after the crew lost situational awareness during a non-precision twin locator approach, killing one passenger. The other 46 passengers and four crew members survived, leaving the aircraft through a breach in the fuselage. The probable cause of the crash was the wrong interpretation of the altimeter readings.

On 9 May 1987, LOT Flight 5055, bound from Warsaw to New York, crashed in the Kabaty forest near Warsaw-Okęcie airport, killing all 172 passengers and 11 crew members, making it the deadliest accident in the history of the airline and the country. The number 2 engine of the Ilyushin Il-62 (SP-LBG) exploded, igniting a fire in the cargo hold and irreparably damaging all but one of the aircraft's control systems as debris punctured the aft fuselage. The crew immediately started an emergency descent after shutting down both the number 1 and 2 engines. The crew mistakenly thought the fire was extinguished. They were due to land at Warsaw Modlin Airport, but, still unaware that the fire continued, changed to Warsaw-Okęcie Runway 33 because of better rescue equipment there. The flight started a left turn to Runway 33 but lost control, and the aircraft crashed into a forest. The cause of the accident was the destruction of engine no 2, resulting in disconnection of the longitudinal control system from the control column, cabin depressurisation, damage to the electric system and fire.

On 2 November 1988, LOT Flight 703 had to execute an emergency landing on a field near Rzeszów following an engine failure. One passenger was killed. The other 24 passengers and four crew on board escaped the Antonov An-24 (SP-LTD), but most of them received serious injuries.

On 31 December 1993, a Boeing 737-300ER (SP-LPA), operating Flight 2 from Chicago to Warsaw, received substantial damage to its nose gear in a hard landing incident at Warsaw-Okecie Airport. After an instrument approach to Runway 11, the aircraft touched down on the main wheels. The nose gear then contacted the runway with enough force to break numerous crown stringers and damage the nose gear assembly. Following this (and two similar 767 accidents in 1992 and 1993), Boeing initiated production modifications to strengthen the upper crown portion of the fuselage.

On 1 November 2011, a Boeing 767-300ER (SP-LPC), operating Flight 16 from Newark Liberty Airport to Warsaw Chopin Airport reported the failure of the hydraulic system that operated the flaps and landing gear. When the back-up system was activated, only the flaps were operable. All attempts to lower the landing gear failed, including one last attempt to use gravity, forcing a gear-up landing on Runway 33 at Warsaw Chopin. The aircraft was written off.

On 10 January 2018, a Bombardier Dash 8 Q400 (SP-EQG), operating a flight from Kraków to Warsaw, reported landing gear issues. The airport was shut down for four hours after an emergency landing. There were no injuries reported.

Hijackings

During the Cold War, when Europe was divided by the Iron Curtain, several LOT aircraft were hijacked and forced to land in Western countries, predominantly in West Germany and especially in West Berlin, owing to it being situated like an island in the Eastern Bloc. The hijackers were usually not prosecuted there but could claim political asylum along with all other passengers who wished to do so.[2]

On 16 September 1949, five armed people forced a LOT flight from Gdańsk to Łódź to divert to Nyköping in Sweden. The Poles were armed with four loaded guns and a toy pistol.

On 16 December 1949, another aircraft on the same route was hijacked and diverted to Bornholm Airport in Denmark. Of the 15 passengers and three crew members on board, 16 decided to claim political asylum.

On 16 October 1969, a LOT Antonov An-24 (SP-LTK) was hijacked by two passengers en route from Warsaw to East Berlin and forced to divert to Berlin Tegel Airport in West Berlin.

On 19 October 1969, a LOT Ilyushin IL-18B was hijacked on its flight from Warsaw to Brussels via Berlin Schönefeld Airport. The aircraft was made to land at Berlin Tegel airport. Both hijackers were from East Germany and requested asylum in West Berlin.

On 20 November 1969, a LOT Antonov An-24 was hijacked on a flight from Wrocław to Bratislava when two passengers forced the pilots to land at Vienna International Airport.

On 5 June 1970, a LOT Antonov An-24 with 24 people on board was hijacked during a flight from Szczecin to Gdańsk and forced to land at Copenhagen Airport, where police forces stormed the aircraft and arrested the perpetrator, who demanded political asylum.

On 9 June 1970, a LOT flight from Katowice to Warsaw was hijacked, but the two people involved were overpowered.

On 7 August 1970, one passenger on board a LOT Antonov An-24 flying from Szczcin to Katowice forced the pilots to divert to Germany. As he did not specify his demands any further, the aircraft landed at Berlin Schönefeld Airport in East Berlin and he was arrested.

On 19 August 1970, five passengers on board an Ilyushin Il-14 en route from Gdańsk to Warsaw forced the pilots to divert to Bornholm Airport in Denmark.

On 26 August 1970, three persons on board a LOT Antonov An-24 en route from Katowice to Warsaw demanded to be taken to Austria. The pilots returned the aircraft to Katowice instead, where the perpetrators were arrested.

On 4 November 1976, a Tupolev Tu-134 (SP-LHD) was forced by two passengers using a dummy bomb to leave its scheduled route from Copenhagen to Warsaw and land at Vienna International Airport instead, where they surrendered to local police forces.

On 24 April 1977, a LOT Tupolev Tu-134 (SP-LGA) was hijacked on a flight from Kraków to Nuremberg in West Germany. The pilots returned to Kraków Airport where the aircraft was stormed, and the hijacker arrested.

On 18 October 1977, an Antonov An-24 (SP-LTH) en route from Katowice to Warsaw was hijacked. Hijackers attempted to force the aircraft to Vienna but were foiled by the crew.

On 30 August 1978, a Tupolev Tu-134 (SP-LGC) operating Flight 165 from Gdańsk to East Berlin was hijacked by two East German citizens armed with starter pistols. They demanded to land at Berlin Tempelhof Airport in West Berlin. Apart from the hijackers, another six people decided to claim political asylum.

On 4 December 1980, an Antonov An-24 (SP-LTB) was hijacked during a flight from Zielona Gora to Warsaw and forced to land at Berlin Tegel Airport. The hijacker was armed with what appeared to be a hand grenade. Upon landing, the hijacker was taken into custody by West Berlin authorities. He requested political asylum and was sentenced to four years in prison for air piracy.

On 10 January 1981, the same aircraft as above was involved in another hijacking attempt. During a flight from Katowice to Warsaw, four passengers demanded to be taken to a Western country. They were armed with sticks of dynamite. They were convinced by the crew that it would be necessary to land and refuel before flying beyond Warsaw. After about an hour of negotiation on the ground, all passengers and crew except the pilot and a flight attendant were permitted to deplane. The hijackers were convinced that it would be easier to switch to another aircraft instead of refuelling the aircraft they were on. As the hijackers moved from one aircraft to the other, they were overpowered and taken into custody by Polish authorities.

On 21 July 1981, an Antonov An-24 (SP-LTI) was forced to land at Tempelhof Airport after having been hijacked during a flight from Katowice to Gdańsk.

On 5 August 1981, the same aircraft was involved in another hijacking attempt while it was flying from Katowice to Gdańsk, but the perpetrator who threatened to blow up the aircraft with explosives was restrained and arrested upon landing at Gdańsk Airport.

On 11 August 1981, another hijacking attempt on the Katowice to Gdańsk route was foiled. While en route, the hijacker held a knife to the throat of a female passenger and demanded to be flown to West Berlin. By changing directions several times, the pilot tricked the hijacker into thinking they had landed there. In fact, the Antonov An-24 (SP-LTT) landed in Warsaw, where the police boarded and took the hijacker into custody.

On 22 August 1981, an Antonov An-24 (SP-LTC), en route from Wrocław to Warsaw, was hijacked. About five minutes after take-off, the hijacker removed a hand grenade from the rear of a portable radio, went to the cockpit and ordered the crew to fly to Tempelhof Airport. After landing in Berlin, the hijacker surrendered to American authorities. He was later turned over to German authorities. He was sentenced by a West Berlin court to five years in prison.

On 18 September 1981, another Antonov An-24 was hijacked. About ten minutes after take-off, a man grabbed a female passenger and held a razor blade to her neck. Eight other men and three women broke bottles and brandished them in a threatening manner toward the crew. They demanded to fly to West Berlin. A Soviet Mil Mi-8 helicopter tried to intercept the aircraft before landing at Tegel Airport but failed to do so. In Berlin, the hijackers surrendered to American authorities and were later turned over to German authorities in West Berlin. They were sentenced variously to one to four years in prison by West Berlin courts.

On 22 September 1981, four passengers tried to hijack an Antonov An-24 (SP-LTK) on a flight from Warsaw to Koszalin. They brandished sharp instruments and threatened a flight attendant. The pilot agreed to their demands but returned to Warsaw. After peaceful means failed, police shot and wounded one of the hijackers and forcefully took the others into custody.

On 29 September 1981, one hijacker demanded an Antonov AN-12 (SP-LTP) on a flight from Warsaw to Szczecin to be diverted to West Berlin. Because more passengers than manifested were aboard the aircraft, police boarded to check. The hijacker put a razor to the neck of another passenger and demanded to be flown to West Berlin. The other passengers threatened the hijacker, and he moved to the rear of the aircraft, where he was arrested.

On 30 April 1982, eight passengers forced an Antonov An-24 (SP-LTG) on a flight from Wrocław to Warsaw to divert to Berlin Tegel Airport. They had overpowered and disarmed the six security men aboard, two of whom were injured. Upon landing, the hijackers were taken into custody by American authorities and turned over to West Berlin authorities. They requested political asylum. Reportedly, 28 other passengers chose to remain in West Berlin. The aircraft, crew, security personnel and remaining passengers were allowed to return to Poland. The hijackers were sentenced to terms ranging from two to four years for endangering air traffic.

On 9 June 1982, two hijackers on board a LOT flight from Katowice to Warsaw demanded to divert the aircraft to West Berlin. Instead, the aircraft landed in Poland, and the perpetrators were arrested.

On 25 August 1982, two passengers forced a flight from Budapest to Warsaw that was operated using an Ilyushin Il-18 (SP-LSI) to divert to Munich Riem Airport. They carried packages that they claimed were bombs. Upon landing at Munich, they were taken into custody. Reportedly, the packages did not contain explosives.

On 22 November 1982, one of three security guards aboard the flight from Wrocław to Warsaw demanded that the aircraft – an Antonov An-24 (SP -LTK) – be flown to West Berlin. Shortly after landing at Tempelhof Airport, the hijacker jumped off the aircraft. He was fired at by the other security guards and was wounded in the right foot. He returned the fire, but no one was hit. He was taken into custody by American officials and later turned over to West German authorities. Four other passengers requested political asylum.

On 25 February 1993, a man forced his way into a LOT ATR 72 (SP-LFA) at Rzeszów Jasionka Airport during the boarding process for Flight 702 to Warsaw, threatening to detonate a hand grenade. Police special forces stormed the aircraft, in which there was a total number of 30 people at the time of the assault. The perpetrator (who proved to be unarmed) was shot at and arrested.

LOT Polish Airlines Fleet Details

(Based upon information from the airline and from Planespotters.net)

Historical Fleet

Aircraft Type	Total Number Used	First Introduction	Last Removed from Fleet
Junkers F 13	15	1929	1936
Fokker F.VII/1m	6	1929	1936
Fokker F.VII/3m	13	1929	1936
Lublin R-XVI	1	1932	1932
PZL.4	1	1933	1935
PWS-24	5	1932	1939
Douglas DC-2	3	1935	1939
Junkers JU 52/3	1	1936	1939
Lockheed L10 Electra	?	1936	1939
Lockheed L14 Super Electra	?	1938	1940
PZL.44 Wicher	1	1939	1939
Lisunov Li-2	40	1945	1969
Douglas DC-3	9	1946	1959
Cessna UC-78 training	14	1946	1950
SNCASE SE.161 Languedoc	4	1947	1950
Ilyushin Il-12B	6	1949	1957
Aero Ae-45	3	1952	1957
Ilyushin Il-14P	4	1955	1961
Convair 240	4	1957	1966
PZL.12	1	1961	1962
Ilyushin Il-18	9	1961	1990
Vickers Viscount	3	1962	1967
Antonov An-24	26	1966	1991
Tupolev Tu-134	5	1968	1994
Tupolev Tu-134A	7	1968	1994
Ilyushin Il-62	7	1972	1992

Aircraft Type	Total Number Used	First Introduction	Last Removed from Fleet
Antonov An-26	?	1974	?
Yakovlev Yak-40		1982	1989
Tupolev Tu-154	?	1986	1995
Douglas DC-8-62	1	1987	1988
Boeing 767-200ER	3	1989	2008
Boeing 767-300ER	7	1990	2013
ATR 72	10	1991	2014
Boeing 737-500	12	1992	2013
Boeing 737-400	10	1993	2020
McDonnell Douglas DC-10-30	3	1994	1996
Boeing 737-300	4	1996	2005
Embraer 145	14	1999	2011
ATR 42	13	2002	2013
Embraer ERJ-170	4	2004	2015
Embraer ERJ-175	4	2006	2017
Fokker 100	?	2016	2016
Bombardier CRJ700ER	2	2016	2020
Bombardier CRJ900ER	12	2016	2020
Boeing 737-700	1	2019	2020
Boeing 737-800	1	2019	2020

Current Fleet

Aircraft type	Total Number	First Delivery
Boeing 737 MAX 8	5	2017
Boeing 737-800	6	2017
Boeing 787-8	8	2012
Boeing 787-9	7	2018
Bombardier DHC-8-400	12	2015
Embraer ERJ-170	6	2004
Embraer ERJ 175	10	2006
Embraer ERJ-190	4	2018
Embraer 195	15	2011

Notes and References

Chapter 1
1. 'Poland', en.wikipedia.org.
2. 'Free City of Danzig', en.wikipedia.org.
3. 'Luftverkehr in Danzig', de.wikipedia.org.
4. Hetman, Karol Placha, 'The History of LOT Polish Airlines Part 14', www.polot.net/en.
5. 'Aerolot', en.wikipedia.org.
6. Hetman, Karol Placha, 'The first air connections in the Republic of Poland', www.polot.net/en.

Chapter 2
1. Stroud, John, 'Wings of Peace – Polish Transports', *Aeroplane Monthly*, June 1991.
2. Hetman, Karol Placha, 'The first air connections in the Republic of Poland', www.polot.net/en.
3. Stroud, John, 'Wings of Peace – Polish Transports', *Aeroplane Monthly*, June 1991.
4. 'Lublin R-XVI', en.wikipedia.org.
5. 'PZL.4', en.wikipedia.org.
6. 'Stroud, John, 'Wings of Peace – Polish Transports', *Aeroplane Monthly*, June 1991.
7. 'PWS 24', en.wikipedia.org.

Chapter 3
1. Hetman, Karol Placha, 'The first air connections in the Republic of Poland', www.polot.net/en.
2. Ibid.
3. Ibid.
4. Ibid.

Chapter 4
1. Hetman, Karol Placha, 'The first air connections in the Republic of Poland', www.polot.net/en.'PZL.12', en.wikipedia.org.
2. Hetman, Karol Placha, 'The history of LOT Polish Airlines Part 1', www.polot.net/en.
3. Ibid.

Chapter 5
1. 'Wladyslaw Gomulka', en.wikipedia.org.
2. 'Edward Gierek', en.wikipedia.org.
3. Ibid.
4. 'Jaruzelski', en.wikipedia.org.

Chapter 7
1. Hetman, Karol Placha, 'The history of LOT Polish Airlines Part 2', www.polot.net/en.
2. Ibid.
3. 'History of LOT', LOT.com.
4. 'Eurolot', en.wikipedia.org.

5. Hetman, Karol Placha, 'The history of LOT Polish Airlines Part 2', www.polot.net/en.
6. 'Swissair', en.wikipedia.org.

Chapter 8

1. Hetman, Karol Placha, 'The history of LOT Polish Airlines Part 2', www.polot.net/en.
2. 'Centralwings', en.wikipedia.org.
3. 'Air Italy Polska Airlines', www.airitalypolska.com.pl.

Chapter 9

1. 'Smolensk Air Disaster', en.wikipedia.org.
2. Bozyk, Piotr, 'LOT: Permission to fly over Siberia', Pasazer.com, 16 November 2011.
3. Krzeminski, Jacek, 'What would happen if LOT went bankrupt?', Obserwator Finansowy.pl, 21 December 2012.
4. Ibid.
5. Morrell, Peter S, Dr, *Airline Finance*, Ashgate Publishing Ltd, October 2012.
6. Krzeminski, Jacek, 'What would happen if LOT went bankrupt?', Obserwator Finansowy.pl, 21 December 2012.
7. Ibid.
8. *State Aid: Commission finds sale of LOT Polish Airlines' subsidiaries did not involve State Aid,* European Commission, Press Release, 20 November 2012.
9. *LOT pursues new 'east meets west' strategy ahead of the 1H2012 privatisation*, CAPA Centre for Aviation, 14 June 2011.

Chapter 10

1. *LOT pursues new 'east meets west' strategy ahead of the 1H2012 privatisation*, CAPA Centre for Aviation, 14 June 2011.
2. Karp, Gregory, 'LOT Polish Airlines is the first airline to announce it will offer a Chicago O'Hare flight aboard a revolutionary Boeing 787 Dreamliner', *Chicago Tribune*, 28 March 2012.
3. *LOT pursues new 'east meets west' strategy ahead of the 1H2012 privatisation*, CAPA Centre for Aviation, 14 June 2011.
4. Easton, Adam and Dombey, Daniel, 'Turkish Airlines eyes LOT purchase', *Financial Times*, 23 January 2012.
5. El Caidi, Sarah, 'Turkish Airlines intéressée par LOT', *Le Journal de l'aviation*, 26 January 2012.
6. *Poland's LOT and Turkish Airlines highlight Eastern European flag carriers investor/seller shortfall,* CAPA Centre for Aviation, 27 January 2012.
7. Gosling, Tim, 'Turkish Airlines drops LOT bid', *bne IntellNews*, 4 June 2012.
8. 'Turkish Airlines pulls out of LOT purchase', *Hürriyet Daily News*, 4 June 2012.
9. 'Turkish Airlines pulls out of LOT partnership plans', *Warsaw Business Journal*, 4 June 2012.
10. Krzeminksi, Jacek, 'What would happen if LOT went bankrupt?', Obserwator Finansowy.pl, 21 December, 2012.
11. Cienski, Jan, 'LOT of aid keeps Polish airline aloft', *Financial Times*, 16 December 2012.
12. 'Polish Airlines to resume flights of Boeing 787 Dreamliners on June 1', *CTV News/Associated Press*, 29 May 2013.
13. Cienski, Jan, 'LOT on: losses and layoffs add to privatisation plan for Polish airlines', *Financial Times*, 14 February 2013.
14. *State Aid: Commission approves restructuring aid for LOT Polish Airlines,* European Commission Press Release, 29 July 2014.

Chapter 11

1. 'LOT Polish Airlines announces 2014 profit on core business', PRNewswire.com, 15 April 2015.
2. Bhaskara, Vinay, 'LOT Polish Airlines aims for sustainable profitability and restructure', Airwaysnews.com, 22 May 2014.
3. Dwyer-Lindgren, Jeremy, 'LOT Polish has reached a deal with Boeing on compensation for its 787 Dreamliner problems', Airwaysnews.com, 12 February 2014.
4. Bhaskara, Vinay, 'LOT Polish Airlines eyes up-gauge to 737 MAX and A320neo and Touts 787 Improvement', Airwaysnews.com, 3 June 2014.
5. 'LOT', Luchtvaartnieuws.nl, 2 April 2015.
6. Cybulak, Pawel, 'LOT and Eurolot on one ticket', Pasazer.com, 15 July 2014.
7. *NIK on the restructuring of PLL LOT*, Supreme Audit Office Poland, 12 April 2016.

Chapter 12

1. 'LOT Polish Airlines capacity up 20% in 2016 but still behind Ryanair in Poland, US routes key to growth in 2017 as fleet will reach 50 aircraft', Anna.Aero, 19 October 2016.
2. *'Nordica and LOT Polish Airlines to launch strategic cooperation'*, Nordica Press Center, 4 November 2016.
3. Coffre, Alain, 'LOT se développe en Estonie', businesstravel.fr, 8 November 2016.
4. Sowinski, Krzysztof, 'Analysis of LOT's financial results for 2017', Pasazar.com, 23 July 2018.
5. 'LOT Polish Airlines', en.wikipedia.org.

Chapter 13

1. Stefan, Teodor,' LOT Polish Airlines profitable in 2019 and record number of passengers', Aeronewsglobal.com, 10 January 2020.
2. Orban, André, 'LOT with profit and record number of passengers in 2019', Aviation24.be, 2 October 2020.
3. 'Lot Polish Airlines' 2019 financial results at last year's level: CEO', tvpworld.com, 22 July 2019.
4. 'New Central Polish Airport', en.wikipedia.org.
5. 'Nordica', en.wikipedia.org.
6. Wissenbach, Ilona, and Lauer, Klaus, *Polish carrier LOT acquires German airline Condor,* Reuters, 24 January 2020.
7. 'LOT Polish Airlines Owner buys Condor', *CH-Aviation*, 24 January 2020.
8. 'LOT Polish abandons Condor: European airline consolidation on hold', CAPA Centre for Aviation, 16 April 2020.
9. Charpentreau, Clement, 'Germany considers Condor nationalization after Polish sale fails', Aerotime.aero, 2 April 2020.
10. Wilczek, Maria, 'German airline sues Polish state aviation group for abandoned takeover by LOT', notesfrompoland.com, 20 November 2020.
11. Gagulski, Lukasz, 'Polish flag carrier suffers huge loss in 2020 pandemic year', thefirstnews.com, 14 July 2021.
12. Sas, Adriana, 'Financial results of LOT Polish Airlines in Poland 2018-2020', Statista.com, 4 October 2021.
13. 'State aid: Commission approves £650 million Polish support to LOT in context of the coronavirus outbreak', European Commission press release, 22 December 2020.
14. 'Over a billion PLL LOT losses for 2020', forsal.pl, 14 July 2021.
15. 'Loss in 2020: The airline's financial results', *Pilne Business Insider Polska*, 14 July 2021.

Chapter 14

1. Orban, André, 'LOT Polish Airlines sells its 49% stake in Xfly to Nordica', Aviation24.be, 31 December 2020.
2. 'LOT Polish Airlines sues Boeing over MAX grounding', Ch-Aviation.com, 28 October 2021.
3. 'LOT verklagt Boeing – und prüft Airbus flotte', *Flug Revue*, 27 October 2021.
4. Fabinger, Jakov, 'LOT Polish Airlines is keen to claim compensation from Boeing', Simpleflying.com, 4 October 2021.
5. 'LOT Chief operating officer on fleet, MRO and sustainability', Aviation Week Network, 6 October 2021.
6. Casey, David, 'Airline in Focus: LOT', Routesonline.com, 23 April 2021.
7. 'LOT Polish Airlines had 4.2 million passengers in 2021', CIJeurope.com, 4 February 2022.
8. Ibid.
9. Orban, André, 'LOT Polish Airlines resumes flights to Miami and to Colombo, Sri Lanka', Aviation24.be, 12 December 2021.
10. Orban, André, 'In September this year, LOT will take off from Warsaw to Dubai', Aviation24.be, 28 April 2021.
11. Casey, David, 'Route analysis: Warsaw-Dubai', Routesonline.com, 27 August 2021.
12. Orban, André, 'LOT to resume flights from Budapest Airport to New York JFK in June', Aviation24.be, 5 January 2022.
13. Mojak, Monika, 'Polish flag carrier LOT suspends flights to Minsk', Euractiv.com, 26 May 2021.
14. 'LOT Polish airlines may lead new airline for Poland, Czech, Hungary and Slovakia', CAPA Center for Aviation, 3 October 2020.
15. 'Airlines face up to rising fuel costs', *Daily Memo*, Aviation Week Network, 1 February 2022.

Appendix 1

1. Semczuk, Przemysław, 'Forgotten flight to Beirut', Newsweek Polska, 2011.
2. 'LOT Polish Airlines', en.wikipedia.org.

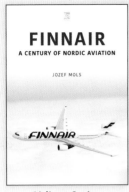

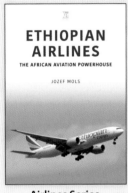